COMING TO JAKARTA

ALSO BY PETER DALE SCOTT

Books

The War Conspiracy: The Secret Road to the Second Indochina War. Bobbs Merrill.

Crime and Cover-Up: The CIA, the Mafia, and the Dallas-Watergate Connection. With a foreword by Sylvia Meagher. Westworks.

Rumors of No Law: Poems from Berkeley 1968-1977. Thorp Springs Press.

Books Written in Collaboration

Education at Berkeley. Report of the Select Committee on Education, Academic Senate. University of California Press.

Franz Schurmann, Peter Dale Scott, and Reginald Zelnik. *The Politics of Escalation in Vietnam.* Beacon Press & Fawcett Premier Books.

Zbigniew Herbert. *Selected Poems.* Translated from the Polish by Czeslaw Milosz and Peter Dale Scott. Ecco Press.

Peter Dale Scott, Paul L. Hoch, and Russell Stetler (eds.) *The Assassinations: Dallas and Beyond—A Guide to Cover-Ups and Investigations.* Random House & Vintage Books.

Jonathan Marshall, Peter Dale Scott, and Jane Hunter. *The Iran-Contra Connection: Secret Teams and Covert Operations in the Reagan Era.* South End Press.

Miscellaneous

"Exporting Military-Economic Development: America and the Overthrow of Sukarno, 1965-67." In Malcolm Caldwell (ed.), *Ten Years' Military Terror in Indonesia.* Spokesman Books, Nottingham.

"The United States and the Overthrow of Sukarno, 1965-1967." *Pacific Affairs* (Vancouver, B.C., Summer 1985).

"The Vietnam War and the CIA-Financial Establishment." In Mark Seldon (ed.), *Remaking Asia: Essays on the American Uses of Power.* Bobbs Merrill.

COMING TO JAKARTA

a poem about terror

Peter Dale Scott

A NEW DIRECTIONS BOOK

Manufactured in the United States of America.

First published clothbound and as New Directions Paperbook 672 in 1989.

New Directions Books are printed on acid-free paper.

This U.S. edition is published by arrangement with McClelland & Stewart, Toronto, Canada, who first issued *Coming to Jakarta* in 1988.

Library of Congress Cataloging-in-Publication Data

Scott, Peter Dale.
    Coming to Jakarta.
    I. Title.
PR9199.3.S364C6   1989   811'.54   88-29125
ISBN 0-8112-1094-4 (alk. paper)
ISBN 0-8112-1095-2 (pbk. : alk. paper)

New Directions Books are published for James Laughlin
by New Directions Publishing Corporation
80 Eighth Avenue, New York 10011

For my father Frank
(1899–1985)

COMING TO JAKARTA

I.i

There are three desks in my office
              at one I read Virgil's
        descent into the underworld

at one I try to sort out
              clippings of failed Swiss banks
        or of slow killings on meat-hooks

in a well-guarded Chicago garage
              but the third desk this one
        is where the typewriter

stares at me with only
              a sheet of white paper
        from which my blank mind

is averted with an
              unmistakable almost
        diamagnetic force

as the page blurs
              to the size of a movie screen
        watched by a captive amphitheater

of all the letters there are
              containing among them every poem
        the mean vaults at the back of my head

would rather kill me than let go of
       so I turn back now
    to mock them: *Mosaic darkness*

constellations of the gulf's floor
          naked half-limbs swift
     alpine cloudburst hail and you

wind-driven ghost of snow
          down the side of the dark
     oak outside my childhood window

with the blind flapping all night
          Why are you here?
     Have you something to tell me?

                  I.ii

In Watertown Massachusetts
          at two in the morning
     the light Canadian novel does not help

to calm the unsteady trees outside
          that have somehow become too much
     part of my being

or the uprising in my stomach
          against so much good food and
     wine America or was it

giving one last broadcast too many
          about the Letelier assassins
     the heroin traffic

a subject I no longer hope
          to get a handle on
     and want so much to vacate

till I think of Noam
        the East Timor massacres
    he cannot publish

or was it those grim
        pre-election faces on campus
    Prepare to meet thy God

still visible under their
        freshly painted ten-foot-high
    VOTE REAGAN banners or just

tonight's vigil with Henrik and Jerry
        in the new bar off Harvard Square
    in the unused freedom of our

Halloween Nixon masks
        unable to decide between
    so many beautiful strangers

I think if I am sick now
        and cannot catch my 9:30 a.m. plane
    will I lose hold forever

of this thin bright
        thread of my particular life
    which hovers here in front

of me like an apparition
        before I get it into
    perspective leading trimly but

without forgiveness through
        the Delta departure gate?
    By its flicker I discern

the surly rebellious trees
        beyond the muttering window
    (the maples of course of my childhood

but no more full of branches
   and black openings than
  the laurels out in California)

have always concealed voices
   too low and too obscene to be heard
  except as revelations

like that face at lunch
   surging with visionary insight
  as J smiled at me

and brought his glass down again
   on the marble tabletop
  too dangerously hard

or like the call from D
   with God's telephone number
  who from exhilaration

stripped for his angels
   in the Safeway parking lot
  and was held by the police

till they learned he was famous
   of course of course
  what are we if not haunted

between these temples
   this world never more full
  of immanent and transcendent glory

than when it rises up over our heads
   the future the one thing
  that cannot escape us

in front of our clumsy hands

I.iii

Taking off the
             plane tilts nearby Cape Cod
        into a map

of when I was eleven
             before it heads north safely
        above the clouds my

hand on the furtively sipped
             ginger ale can relaxes
        I look down without nausea

on the invisible peaks
             the stewardess is walking over
        as if minutes not sweaty years

separated them all Chocorua
             where I first broke out
        above a tree-line Washington

my head pounding with the fake
             clairvoyance of altitude
        Lafayette where silhouetted strangers

led us back down through
             the dense surprise blizzard
        to the festive safety

of the Dartmouth Outing Club hut
             Already we are descending
        into these shadows which

hang about as if there
             were something much more urgent
        left wholly unsaid and we

cross the supposed
            parallel which separates
      the Vermont end of Lake

Memphremagog from Owl's Head
            or Lake Massawippi my protected
      childhood summers *the true north*

The descent is bottomless
            even after I step out
      at Dorval Airport

strengthened by the sure
            pavement the one
      November snowflake on my lapel

I listen to my *un taxi*
                  s'vous plêt and the
      comfort of this exotic

self unused for two decades
            relaxes or jolts me still further
      out of space into untidy

time which cannot be just
            flown over but engulfs us
      I am piloted by the Greek

immigrant taximan
            through the departed woods of
      what was once the Côte de Liesse

towards my seventy-four-year-old mother
            my father who is eighty-one
      and I am so released

as to forget tomorrow
            I will again be airborne
      losing hold seems for one moment

to be no threat
           but another beginning in
       the long voyage home

to where
we have never been

II.i

We circle and are circling
            in this planet of cloud
        on the other side of this too small

window beats the weather
            we cannot feel
        the old problem of ontological

insufficiency of having
            no answer to *Who am I?*
        no there there

yet the plane always delivers
            some illusion of landing
        scheduled soon to be the mists

of California
            the typewriter
        I am at home with

not the bare elm
            I stare through in our backyard
        as I did in the war years

towards the house of the childhood
            neighbor I would blush to meet
        after she left her blind up

but the beads of light
        on the twigs and now dancing
     water above my head did I

nearly drown once yes
        it was the summer
     Harry and I were trapped

under the rowboat
        we had tipped on purpose
     now closing us in as if

with its own animal will
        till I cannot breathe
     and suddenly to my relief

I am back on the lake
        the lake I will write about
     the complacent water

mindlessly sheening itself
        under our wharf
     where I stare down deep between the boards and see

beyond distorted caricatures of self
        green furtive shadows
     the slime of bottom weed

and among the dim stones
        the blind crawlings
     not willingly remembered

the warped plank pressing my cheekbone
        I begin to discern how
     to my relief this is to be

beyond the confines of my mind
a poem about terror

II.ii

Not that one could imagine
        at this lake and its village
    either belonging or escape

no virgin forest
        all the land private
    except when my father took me

down to the unclaimed camp
        in the pines of Black Point
    cold water slapping

the underside of the canoe
        away from the large outboards
    the still more expensive sailboats

we slip by the sagging
        mostly closed-up boathouses
    of the American estates

or rarely catch them
        with their bright awnings out
    the grass mown to the birch at the water's edge

Years later when Joan
        unlocked the door to the yellow cottage
    above Fisher's Point

entering with a candle
        because the windows were shuttered
    and the power off

as we inhaled the damp
        staining the Bartlett prints
    the mouse droppings among the blue china

it was that rare privilege
of invading a space
long vivid in imagination

and I think now of so many
sinister uninhabited houses
the white swords of glass

I had to pay for although
I said I only went along
with those rich American strangers

I had met on Cape Ann
Think for yourself my mother said
above all the unlocked screen

in the vacant Westmount mansion
where just that once we boys
and girls went in to play goose

the search over Aileen's
too solid body
as Roger whispered

outrageous urgings in my ear
to no avail not yet
knowledgeable enough

for that dark secret
I went downstairs
to play Beethoven

faster and fiercer than ever
on the absent stranger's piano
all of us excited

not belonging there
we could do anything
we never went back

never again the same gang
            yet it seems now
        natural compared to that room

adorned as I had suspected
            with an authentic nineteenth-
        century primitive landscape

long since stolen
            which we stood in front of as Joan
        told me how her ever-

absent ex-husband worked overseas
            for the CIA or perhaps
        some heavier unnamed agency

II.iii

What I remembered as a child
            was the green country
        all the back roads unpaved

the land once cleared
            not changing much except
        there were too many graveyards

in the fields and sugarbush
            for the number of living
        as if the stream of time

hitting the rock of Quebec
            were somehow deflected leaving
        the millpond in Moe River

where I watched my clothes
            on their willow sandbar
        go under as the sluice closed

or the drafty edifice
            in Waterville of the world's
    last snath factory

near where I rode by sleigh
            to the Compton railway station
    on the lap of the fur-coated gentleman

whose initials *L St L*
            on the gold band of his walking-stick
    next to my left eye

meant he was the local M.P.
            (son of J.B.M.
    Saint-Laurent whose name

was painted in big green letters
            on the general store)
    going up to become Prime Minister

As I grew older I learned
            to catch when the wind was right
    the whiff of sulphite from East Angus

I read of the Magog textile strike
            the year-long fight for the diseased
    miners up in Asbestos

so much more than had met my eye
            when it barely came up to
    Mr. Lebaron's grocery counter

but it was decades after
            we rented our first house
    on the American side

from what Raleigh Elizabeth's father
            called one of the FFV
    the First Families of Virginia

and I thought it was a joke
   even when Lily's cousin
  became Secretary of State

decades after all that
   doing my eccentric research
  into the Vietnam War I

became aware of the Summer Social Register
   read in print of "Kanozas"
"Hillside" "Bond's Adventure"

and saw for the first time
   how Lake Massawippi
  was no ordinary lake

not like Memphremagog ten miles off
   (where T.S.Eliot
  heard his celebrated *Turdus*

drip drop drip drop drop drop drop
   in Quebec County)
  but a lake where even

the names of the mailboxes
   along the American side
  were of a compact so invisible

and seamless as to exclude mere wealth
   except when duly arrived
  and so mistrustful of too high culture

as to exclude Wallace Stevens
   or Eliot himself
  yet admit those whom

I remember as
   red-faced tennis players
  slamming their angry racquets

at the Club
         It is at this moment
         rising up as if in a small plane

I see what I have to do

                    II.iv

I am writing this poem
         about the 1965 massacre
         of Indonesians by Indonesians

which in an article ten years later
         I could not publish
         except in Nottingham England with

a friend Malcolm Caldwell who has since
         himself been murdered   *Becker 433-36*
         no one will say by whom but I will guess

seeing as this is
         precisely poetry
         the CIA's and now Peking's Cambodian

assassins the Khmer Serai
         In that article I estimated
         a *half-million or more*

killed in this period   *P.D. Scott '75 209*
         it took Noam in a book
         suppressed by its first publisher

to quote Admiral Sudomo
         of the Indonesian junta
         more than 500,000

and now Amnesty International
     many more than one million
   so much for my balanced prose

Chomsky 208

But none of us experienced
     that pervasive smell of death
   those impassable rivers

clogged with corpses
     Robert Lowell is that why
   even you a pacifist

had so little to say about it?
     Or you gentle reader
   let us examine carefully

the good reasons
     you and I
   don't enjoy reading this

Like the time
     in the steep Engadine
   we saw the silent avalanche

fall away from the mountain
     hair and eyebrows
   the first to feel

the murmurations
     of the spreading
   killer wind

II.v

It takes a barbarian to recognize
     the fallibility and splendor
   of a capital

which is why you EP   *Ezra Pound*
            out of Idaho and Wyncote
        only son of an only son

at the Homeric no man's second
            when London and Paris let you down
        took as better friends

Guido and Arnaut
            dawnlight in apricot blossom
        above the massive basilica

lodged in the narrow valley
            for eight hundred years
        e lo soleils plovil   *and the sun rains*

to inhabit the past and future
            not as an evasion
        but to maintain the dialect

and as for the mirror of T'ai Tsung
            who endowed the T'ang poets and
        was felicitous in his assassins

or the fountainhead of Justinian
            whom Procopius records
        as the depopulator of Cisalpine Gaul

and whose gratuitous
            destruction of the Gothic kingdom
        opened the Po to the Lombards

what Pope Gregory
            saw not as portent but as
        fulfilment of the world's end

you had read in Dante
            trust them even as gods
        and looked for guidance to the state

so little light I cannot
            blame you who endured
      the corruption of the republic

but as for your love of splendor
            which is to say subjection
      you were too dazzled for the

muzzy language of the *damn bhuddists*
            until they put you in the wind and rain
      and Kuanon upheld you

and the leaves' tapestry
            your voice broken with authority
      As to what haunts us

the ant's forefoot
            you knew best master
      and it was hopeful your net

of fishermen's glass globes
            Kung and Eleusis
      was botched in places

wrong-headed
            so little light
      you had read the best books

and they did not save you
            it has not yet been from truth
      we have gone into war

and I was moved to reject
            the blind man's prophecy
      Odysseus

shalt lose all companions

II.vi

One of those wartime summers
        I spent ten miles to the east
    in the village of Compton

with my cousin Rosemary
        haying a little
    and working in the orchards

the trees so overladen
        their limbs seemed
    to tell us by their gestures

of relief at being picked
        no men for the harvest
    that is what the war meant

to the Eastern Townships
        and otherwise
    I would not have felt

my mind simplify
        as the deepening glow
    of gold from the polished winesaps

signalled the slow approach
        of suppertime
    the good ache knotting my shoulders

and then evening
        the village of Compton
    the whole Coaticook valley

quiet as in winter
        with the roads closed by snow
    why shouldn't everyone

be able to do this
    I said then and still
   say it no matter how hard

it was later priming
    in the tobacco field
   or keeping up with the horse-drawn boat

while the girls in the shade
    sang Hungarian songs and
   racked the leaves on slats

and after this morning's
    phone call with my mother
   despite the pacifist

refugee nephew of Freud
    above North Hatley
   who asked the trespassers

not to hunt on his land
    until one of them
   came back after lunch

shot him in the back
    and the coroner of the township
   agreed it was accidental

I thought he was a bear

II.vii

It seems that where there is
    tolerance there has always been
  paranoia

I remember my own from the thirties
            when my father was away
        at so many hopeful conferences

on economic democracy
            for which the RCMP
        to my amazement

began to tap our phone
            or on peace and world order
        my first postcard from Yosemite

I could not believe there were
            such high waterfalls
        and after Canberra

a eucalyptus boomerang
            etched with cartoon koalas
        why would anyone

make our phone tick
            or write the rude editorials
        people sent my father

about the Rhodes Scholar network
            On my own I learned of
        the attacks by Joe McCarthy

and the Internal Security Subcommittee
            on professors at Harvard
        like John Fairbank

a consistent backer
            of the Chinese Communists   '52 Hearing 3980
        or on Owen Lattimore

among far eastern specialists
            the principal agent
        of Stalinism according to

his opponent in OSS
        and of course on Alger Hiss
     on Leo Pasvolsky and Isaiah Bowman

the Council on Foreign Relations
        the six-man core group
   which guided the secret

War-Peace Studies
        and also drafted
     the United Nations Charter   *Shoup 153*

Years years later I then
        also reading with mistrust
   the publications of the CFR   *Council on Foreign Relations*

about oil and Southeast Asia
        when in the smallest way I found
   my father's name and Raleigh's

in the IPR Hearings   *Institute of Pacific Relations*
        no more hopeful conferences then
   and no more CCF   *Canadian socialist party*

after the advertising blitz
        in which Gladstone Murray
   the British intelligence veteran

called its leader David Lewis
        Lodz the Polish Jew
   By the time I had finished college

my father was staying at home
        once or twice he lay on the floor
   and talked to the ceiling

but mostly he was just
        getting out of politics
   I am not a swan   *F.R. Scott '86*

and he marked in his Brecht
        we who desired to prepare
        the soil for kindness

could not ourselves be kind   *Hamburger 321*

II.viii

At those wartime Hatley parties
        there was Lily Dulles
    the Jersey Lily

so when I went to Oxford
        I picked out her cousin
      Allen by the family name

years before a Korean bullet
        deDullicized his head
    the *New York Times*

showing the sorrowful father
        bent over the prostrate form
    of his only son   *Mosley 6*

one day before his confirmation
        as CIA director
    A decade after that

I met her niece Marian
        in San Francisco
      who knew my cousin Ibby

and held in her fashionable
        art gallery benefits
      for the Free Speech Movement

we used to dine
            in the mid–sixties
    with Marian's friends

the fast Marin set
            kids of the eastern famous
    until their marriages broke up

radicalized by day
            in the nighttime still black tie
    and then after midnight

the pool in our underwear
            it was in those
    deteriorating days that Lily

whom Marian had brought
            back into my life
    as gracious and

as talkative as ever
            told me in my car
    with its blinkers flashing

next to a hydrant
            outside her hotel
    how hard that family

had been on its sons
            Avery converted Jesuit
    son of Foster

and the untreatable Allen
            who brooded over
    his father's philandering

Mosley 126

his mother's therapy
            in expensive Swiss clinics
    with a disciple of Jung

And Lily told me
        of her childlessness
    it was hardest on the women

so women are fools too
        I shan't deny it
    but those relentless fathers

and I remembered
        how in front of the guests
    on the broad veranda

of a Lake Simcoe estate
        some son-in-law picked up
    the still hot squirrel

which his hound had mangled
        and blooded the face
    of his three-week-old son

or Mosley's account of Allen
        in his mother's clinic
    lashing out at his father

with *a look of absolute hatred*
        I'm never coming home
    to you ever   *Mosley 480*

II.ix

Despite my careful upbringing
        according to the handbooks
    of the post-war twenties

which urged that all family
        interactions be conducted
    in an adult rational manner

when I went back to the Rectory
        of my father's father the Archdeacon
    it pleased me to hear grace

and despite my precocious
        enlightenment about sex
    through a book about pollen and frogs

I still almost tremble
        when I think of those unexpected nights
    in the darkest corner

of my father's study
        reading his *Sexual Life of Savages*
    my introduction to the third world

with its terrifying permissiveness
        licit childhood intercourse
    customary rape

though I have since read
        how often the third world
    has just such fantasies of us

and more terrifyingly
        my introduction also
    to the quite opposite challenge

of a free modern future
        where one must throw off tabus
    This has all come back

from crouching this afternoon
        in the library stack
    with the sepia photographs

of Krause's *Bali*   *Market Scene*
        the *Marktszene* of the young pig
    muzzled and bound with raffia

its flesh clutched to the seller's
         firmly resistant breasts
      as she watches intently

the buyer's eyes free of cheating
         not the hands counting cash
      and later with the same

nostalgic crescendo
         the *Badeszene* the *Frau wäscht sich*   *Bath Scene*
      die Unterarme the *Haarwaschen*   *Woman Washing*
                                              Her Underarms   Hairwashing

from which someone
         of that excited era
      lecher puritan aesthete or all three

has with a razor excised
         page after page in efficient
      oblongs all pairs of breasts

but not the sugary prose *so schön*   *so lovely*
         wie eine Frau   *as a woman*
      nur gedacht werden kann   *can only be imagined*

I have read elsewhere
         how this same market Bangli
      grew from nothing in the nineteenth century

when reached by international trade
         which is to say opium
      at controlled British prices

87 per cent of imports
         at Singaraja in 1859
      the rest mostly Manchester goods

until *by the end of the century*
         nearly every adult Balinese
      male and female was an addict

the smoke
           so dense in the palace
      lizards fell from the walls in a stupor   *Geertz '80 89, 204*

the terrifying power
           of the money economy
      Geertz could not explain

the unfavorable trade balance   *Geertz '80 202*
           it was the old rule
      among Chinese in Sarawak

buy for ten sell for seven
           pay back three
      and keep four   *May 73*

the world like myself
in its unintegrated desires

                    II.x

EP however nuts
           you may have been
      in your Wagnerian way

you were right to talk about banks
           the problem of stored desire
      which becomes no one's

In August 1914
           the State Department
      vetoed J.P. Morgan's loan to France

but the check to trade was so great
           there was risk of depression   *Duroselle 55*
      and with Lansing's approval

                    37

Morgan raised $500 million
          to stabilize the pound
and restore commerce

the German response
          of unlimited submarine warfare
and Wilson's declaration

causing gold to flow to the Federal Reserve
          $83 billion
for the first Liberty Loan

making the U.S. Government
          the world's creditor   *Hudson 6*
an unprecedented debt

Marian's Uncle Bill Bullitt
          on a jaunt to Moscow
with Lincoln Steffens

for the benefit of peace   *Kaplan 245*
          A young man of great heart
said Lenin

but *Sind sie bevollmächtigt?*
          Are you empowered?   *Kaplan 246*
French intelligence

getting the text
          and starting a campaign
I've never known even today

whether Wilson knew about it   *Berle 11*
          Bullitt Berle
Isaiah Bowman all resigning

and with pain I recognize
          from my small vantage point
in the subcommittee of four

disarmament talks
        with lights like Lodge and Moch
     so naive I wrote a memo

to ban atmospheric testing
        Why not peace now
     which Lenin has accepted?   *Bullitt 11*

Or how the Dulles clan
        sensing the historic
     foregathering at the Conference   *Mosley 57*

Allen *a little too free*
        on the Boundary Commission
     with Jules Cambon

of the Banque Paribas
        drawing a red line
     around the Sudetenland

Those were the days
        when we were full
     of a spirit of generosity   *Mosley 61*

When it was over
        it was necessary to write
     of the *wheels within wheels*

connections without coherence
        the President himself
     to say nothing of Lloyd George and Clemenceau

did not begin to know
        all that was going on
     in that cave of winds   *Baker 489; Kaplan 244*

Marian I'm sorry
        that your Uncle Bill
     a real sweetie

lived to persuade Bao Dai
        whose retinue in Hong Kong
     was paid by the Banque de l'Indochine

that he could be head of state
        with American support   *PP I 25*
    I'm sorry that Berle

so kind to my mother-in-law
        after her divorce
     lived to praise Johnson's

decision to intervene
        with U.S. troops
    and save Indonesia

from *the Chinese orbit*
        as *that of a big man*
    a towering figure   *Berle 826*

And as for the Dulles clan

II.xi

EP the year you heard Steffens
        on the lucidity of Lenin   *Stock 278*
     not yet at the end of your tether

after the German mark
        inflated a trillion-fold
     the author of the Dawes plan

to reschedule German reparations
        so that the Allies
     could continue their U.S. payments

was Lansing's young nephew
John Foster Dulles
appointed at J.P. Morgan's request   *Mosley 75*

a brilliant job
until the pyramid of debt
led to the Great Depression

Sullivan and Cromwell
handling much of the legal work
for U.S. loans in Germany

his brother Allen
at the J. Henry Schroder Bank
still closely associated

as it was in the thirties
with Schröder Gebrüder   *Marshall '81 9-11*
though Allen of course testified

his bank had no business with Nazis
in the end it was he not Foster
who saw the Nazi threat

to the global system
arranging for Sullivan and Cromwell
to leave Germany

before Dupont left the firm   *Mosley 92*
and when the partners threatened to resign
Foster capitulating   *Hoopes 47*

as Allen later told it
in tears
a rugged and rather gauche figure

with no interest in art
whose true pleasure
was sailing in rough weather

battling with elements he couldn't control   Hoopes 41
          The unequal distribution
     of natural advantages he wrote

is one of the causes of war   Van Dusen 17; Dulles 58
          an international order
     which by its very nature

is self-destructive and
          a breeder of violent revolt   Hoopes 52
     the search for peace

through the World Council of Churches
          led Foster to oppose
     vengefulness and self-righteousness   Van Dusen 94

although he would live to see
          his colleague Niebuhr
     condemn his self-righteousness

EP when counterintelligence
          threw you in a cage
     you who had never objected

to the wealth of Barney and Cunard
          drew on a compassion
     denied to bankers and lawyers

Foster unforgiven
          for opposing that war
     and at the same time

advising Crowley
          the Alien Property Custodian
     Sullivan and Cromwell

meanwhile representing Halbach
          of the I.G. Farben subsidiary   PM 1/1/45
     still controlled by Schroders

(raw materials for Hitler in London
                a powerful interest   *Time* 7/10/39
        in the victory of Franco

and an end to the proposed   *PM* 3/3/45
            nationalization of the Spanish potash industry)
Van Dusen honors

that spiritual quest
            for *some great creative purpose*   *Van Dusen* 97
    a continuing United Nations

autonomy for subject peoples
            control of military establishments
    religious and intellectual liberty   *Van Dusen* 110

let us run with endurance
the race that is set before us

                    II.xii

In the Vietnam era
            when my best friends were
        always saying *choose*

I produced footnotes on Laos
            in so-called non-
        schismogenic investigation

for my moonlight research
            which got me invited
        to an academic conference

the Concerned Asian Scholars
            in a downtown church
        opposite the San Francisco

Hilton and the AAS   *Association of Asian Studies*
                At its panel on the
        McCarthy era

history inverted itself
                Lillian Hellman and John Fairbank
        on the podium

Lattimore silent in the audience
                this fight among ourselves
        hard questions from the floor

on Fairbank's links to the SSRC   *Social Science Research Council*
                and the Ford Foundation
        after Fairbank's warning

the great danger then and now
        is politicized thinking
either right or left

Maylie and I
                had afternoon tea
        with Wilma Fairbank

which extended towards dinner
                despite my reiterated
        warnings I had to leave

for a nighttime rally
                and TV interview against
        U.S. activities in Laos

in the darkening room
                Wilma talked of Franz Schurmann's
        abandonment of a promising

scholarly career
        for simple journalism
one of John's best students

Heavy-hearted as I sat
              later under the
       bright klieg lights

I could think only of
              an eleven-year-old
       and four adults

canoeing among the
              waterlily pads
       of the upper Charles

hand trailing in the water
              I was allowed to taste
       their twenty-five-cent

California chianti
              as the canoes nosed
       deeper into the rushes

playing hide-and-seek
              no suggestion yet
       of the fall of the Kuomintang

the arms and narcotics traffic
              unmarked planes out of T'ainan   *P.D. Scott '72 204*
       Shig Katayama the Sumatrans   *Sampson '77 239*
                                                                          P.D. Scott '75 215

but only the inveterate
              poet and connoisseur
       Li Po

                    II.xiii

The bankers feared
              that *a German victory*
       would render gold worthless   *Blum '65 109; '70 296*

                          45

the British Treasury had been planning
          to negotiate procurement
     through the Chase National Bank   *Wisely 133*

I thought you were a bank
          Roosevelt said
     I didn't know you were a merchant   *Blum '65 101; '70 293*

None of this in Schurmann
          or William Appleman Williams
     Horowitz most eloquently silent

and in those dog days
          EP you sailed out
     through the Pillars of Heracles

to talk gold and silver
          with Unkle George Tinkham
     who needled Morgenthau

about selling British securities
          If you will pardon
     my saying so

the Secretary answered
          you are probably
     in the minority   *Blum '65 223*

Anxious to avoid
          a family quarrel with Foster
     who complained of Donovan's

crackpot *war hysteria*
          Allen maintained
     only a quiet connection

with Stephenson's New York units   *Mosley 113*
          until after Pearl Harbor
     when head of oss in Berne

he dealt with the Bank
        of International Settlements
    the first World Bank

as well as with Westrick
        his firm's Berlin representative
    and other German contacts from the twenties

for such intelligence coups
        as the Holohan mission
    which you EP

knowing less than even
        the House Armed Services Committee
    called *murder protected*   *Canto 85/559*

or Operation SUNRISE   *R.H. Smith 396; Brown 816*
        the salvaging of Italian Superpower's
    holdings in the Po Valley

on the initiative of a
        Knight of Malta
    representing his father-in-law   *R.H. Smith 114*

(with the help of McCaffery
        of Hambro's and SOE   *Special Operations Executive*
    and the Sindona affidavit)   *Lernoux 189*

and Count Volpi whose *kilowatt energy*   *Canto 80/509*
        Unkle George the isolationist
    observed *at the Lido*   *Canto 76/461*

was Italian Superpower
        and after I told Dick Smith
    the ex-CIA historian

that Allen's OSS boss
        Forgan was another director
    of Italian Superpower

his typescript came back
          with this small detail altered   *R.H. Smith 116*
      into a lie indicating

someone found it significant
          perhaps because SUNRISE
      the German surrender in North Italy

led to Stalin's fury
          and Roosevelt's last assurances
      with *less than convincing candor*   *Kolko 378*

Allen's Jungian mistress
          no doubt oversimplified
      when she said Allen

had come to oust the Nazis
          to make Germany *safe again*
      for the Junkers and Prussians

and of course Sullivan and Cromwell   *Mosley 170*
          but when Foster and Allen agreed
      on the magic formula

to help eliminate Communism   *Mosley 437*
          in Iran Guatemala
      Standard Oil and United Fruit

were not unhappy
          violence
      loving to breed violence

and then *this is something*
          that cannot be in writing
      but I prefer

a break-up of that country
            furnishing a fulcrum
        to help eliminate communism   *Mosley 437; P.D. Scott '85B 212*

Indonesia

                        II.xiv

We must consider the five sons
            of Meyer Rothschild
        whose clearing-houses replaced

the shipping of bullion
            by a world-wide system of accounts
        or what Franz Schurmann called

the most important force
            for peace in the nineteenth century   *Schurmann '74 62*
        and consider Meyer's grandson

Lionel First Baron Rothschild
            who financed the reimbursement
        of slave-owners in the dominions

and the Crimean War
            a break with his anti-war policy
        because the czar was an anti-Semite

The Rothschilds' worst legacy
            was not that dubious boost
        to the failing Ottomans of the Sublime Porte

not the flamboyance
            of Gunnersbury Park
        the wiles of Disraeli

not even their support
of that clean-living young
adventurer Cecil Rhodes

an account not reckoned up until this century
No! it was to have invented this world
that can only be dominated

not yet ready to govern
Lionel who lived by
his grandmother's confidence

War? nonsense
my boys won't let them   Morton 90

II.xv

I always thought of my father
as a radical not like
my grandfather who taught me grace

I was shocked years later
when studying U.S.
economic interests in Southeast Asia

to find he had published
in *Foreign Affairs* the journal
of the Council on Foreign Relations

whose name I first heard
that brilliant afternoon
on Raleigh's Hatley veranda

drinking what may have been champagne
above the sailboats
with the dark-haired Gregor

50

whose father it had been explained
        owned the house
        next to Eloise's by the bandstand

a second cousin of her uncle Harfie
        through the Fishes and Stuyvesants
        blood of two Secretaries of State

and was important the editor
        of *Foreign Affairs*
        and the brains as I read later

behind the War and Peace Studies
        the CFR and State project   *Shoup 119*
        Allen Dulles helped establish

the nature of their work
        precluded them from receiving
        any public remuneration or reward   *Council 24,4*

and because the memos are still secret
        we can only guess
        they proposed the creation of a CIA

Happily ignorant of all this
        I had watched Gregor
        in her white tennis outfit

how I wished I had learned tennis but
        instead I harangued her
        about German socialists

some of whom I had met
        at a six-week student seminar
        mysteriously funded

by a flurry of cold war acronyms
        I read about later
        I have since tried to imagine

describing on that veranda
　　　　the sugary scent on a hot day
　　from the corpses in Hamburg's rubble

how we who had been spared
　　　　unlike young Harfie
　　now smiling from his wheelchair

must think as survivors
　　　　but I do not think our meeting
　　could have come out otherwise

compelled largely from shyness
　　　　to attack the column
　　on an SPD sellout　　　　　　　　　　*Socialist Party of Germany*

in the *Gazette*
　　　　by her stepfather Walter Lippmann
　　whose book just two years earlier

I had carefully underlined
　　　　in the McGill library
　　I challenged her head held high

beside the crabapple blossom
　　　　with the same earnestness
　　as when I underlined my calculus

the intrinsic merits of a question
are not for the public　　　　　　　　　　*Lippmann 144*

II.xvi

As for banks EP
　　　　you who wrote of Schacht
　　London loans to Tibet

the decline of the Adamses
        Sir William Wiseman who financed
    the purchase of the *Chicago News*

so that Knox could preach against
        isolation and for war
    even if you believed

Van Buren's self-serving account
        of how he brought down Biddle
    and the Bank in Philadelphia

to the profit of Taney's
        banking advisers in New York
    and their correspondents the Rothschilds

a shifting of the country's financial center
        from Chestnut Street to Wall Street   *W.B. Smith 204*
    how come in your attacks

on Roosevelt you never once mentioned
        that chief integrator
    of Morgan policies the CFR

the Council on Foreign Relations
        where in 1952
    it was agreed

the Guatemalan government
        was merely carrying out the plan
    laid out for it by Oumansky

according to the study group
        chaired by Spruille Braden
    of State and then United Fruit

Nelson Rockefeller
        knows the situation and
    can work a little with Eisenhower on it   *Shoup 196*

the Council on Foreign Relations
        for whom William Henderson of Mobil
    called Southeast Asia

vitally significant an
        economic and strategic prize   *Shoup 227*
    in those dog-day fifties

when I more suited
        than any bank clerk
    felt honored to meet Dean Rusk

thought Sastroamidjojo boring
        and mimicked the trembling hands
    of Penn Nouth who sat beside me

in the C's of the United Nations
        and whose friends are now all dead
    Henderson called for an *interventionist*

unlimited final commitment   *P.D. Scott '74 127*
        or in the words
    of the CFR-commissioned study

by Russell H. Fifield
        sometime State Department official
    professor of political science

at the University of Michigan
        and the National War College
    Secretary of the Association

of Asian Studies
        a challenge of major proportions   *Fifield 3*
    in which the CIA's clients

who had just been defeated
        in the '58 Sumatra revolt
    could not *be overlooked*

in Indonesia's future
        if only because   P.D. Scott '75 219
    of their rare qualities of leadership   Fifield 312

                    II.xvii

Training and education for leadership
        can be an important
    indirect result

of the U.S. military program   Fifield 102
        wrote Fifield who must have known
    what Ford and the University

of California were up to
        officer corps disciplined
    eager to get things done

anti-Communist in outlook
        attributes of leadership
    not widely found

in Southeast Asia   Fifield 300
        such was the academic
    language of Professor Fifield

not ██ ██████
     ████ █████
        nor I suppose Guy Pauker

another of those jet-lagged
        CFR policy consultants
    a displaced Rumanian

so deferential
        about his quite adequate English
    when we debated Vietnam

before the pitiless Irvine students
      and while on the
         RAND payroll the founder

of an academic center at Berkeley
         where as professor of political science
      he developed the program

to train the cadres of
         SESKOAD the Indonesian
      army command school

of which I knew nothing
         when confused
      by a sudden surge

of my old combativeness
         saying *you*
      political scientists

are part of the problem
         and the students all
      starting to applaud I

hushed them and turned
         to apologize *of course*
      not you personally

I did not know then
         you had publicly castigated
      old friends in

the Indonesian military
         for not *carrying out*
      a control function

for lacking
         the ruthlessness
      that made it possible

for the Nazis to suppress
the Communist Party
a few weeks after the elections

in which the Communist Party   *P.D. Scott '75 231*
won five million votes   *Pauker '64 221-23*

                    II.xviii

I was always going along
            at first with whatever
      sounded most reasonable

and that is why
            in the late fifties
      I would have agreed with John Fairbank

attacked for his love of China
            that to have got $30 million
      through the Social Sciences Research Council

from John Brigham Howard
            international research and training
      director of the Ford Foundation

for academic studies of China
            would be *an important means*
      for bringing it that is to say the

cold war *to an end*   *Fairbank 111*
            and why in the seventies
      I agreed with the CCAS

the Committee of Concerned Asian Scholars
            on the need to investigate
      the considerable correspondence

                                                57

between the aims of the research committee
      set up by John Fairbank
  and what General Dick called

research needs in the social sciences
      relevant to the U.S. Army's
  limited war needs   *Bulletin 92-93*

yet now in the eighties
      this dispute among friends
  who might with a little reflection

have understood each other
      seems less important
  than the discovery it was the Ford

Foundation with MIT
      which first sent Guy Pauker
  to Indonesia and then

$2.5 million to Pauker's students
      for training the officers at SESKOAD
  In the words of John Brigham Howard

whom one learns from *Who's Who*
      was formerly depchief
  of AMAG in Greece   *American Military*
                                          Advisory Group

millions in military aid
      to what even the Twentieth
  Century Fund called rightist terror

Ford felt it was training the guys
      who would be leading the country
  which is to say Indonesia

when Sukarno got out   *Ransom 99; P.D. Scott '75 233*
      and the Ford man in Jakarta
  Michael Harris the former

labor rep in Paris
        when the CIA passed millions
    to split the French labor movement

was said by one member
        of the UC Indonesia project
    to have felt himself superior

to the U.S. Ambassador   *P.D. Scott '85B 216-17*
        in his work with the CIA
    the Asia Foundation

and those whom at first
        I declined to mention   *P.D. Scott '75 255*
    (in our sort of life

people of sound mind
        had to shut their eyes)   *Mandelstam 58*
    whom Pauker called

at the Nugan Hand meeting
        the so-called Berkeley Mafia
    I talked them into coming

to the University
        running the country today
    fun to have around   *Kwitny 310*

with devastating consequences   *Mandelstam 58*

According to the court poets
   of the *Babad Tanah Jawi*
  Agung could have destroyed Batavia

by his occult power
   he had his commander Purbaya
  fly through the air

to make a hole in the wall
   with a thaumaturgical utterance
  and his commander Madureja

whom he knew to be a traitor
   give fight with his troops
  until all were slain

so that the grateful Dutch
   sent envoys to Mataram
  with annual tribute

estimated by Vlekke
   at 60,000 guilders
  in the most expensive year

in exchange for which
   the sultan Agung
  forced the coastal people

to deliver rice and wood
   at no cost to himself
  in forty-one years the company

made a profit of 25 million guilders
   of which 9.7 million
  were remitted to Amsterdam   *May 15-16*

This is how it was
            before the World Bank
      Royal Dutch Shell

the destruction of the rain forests
            8000 species a year
      power and submission

There have always been poets

                  III.ii

To have learnt from terror
            to see oneself
      as part of the enemy

can be a reassurance
                  whatever it is
      arises within us

fear
                  a matter of self-protection
      quick wits in the urban streets

where my parents for socialist reasons
            lived in the thirties
      and my toys reluctantly shared

seemed always to disappear
                  except when I was conducted
      to play alone on the lawn

of the nearby campus
            or dressed up in polished
      gaiters with a buttonhook

to go have tea with Gran
   or Christopher and his maiden aunts
  at the edge of Mount Royal

there were in our house
   so many meetings
  but when my parents hugged

I would get between their knees
   to be *in the carriage*
  I used to be sent out

to play in the snow till lunch
   or until the pack
  of boys took my sled

I recall much blood
   the time I hit Babs
  whom I remember as so gentle

or the broken window
   as black as the lake's bottom
  after I had been chased

one more time behind
   our insecure board fence
  and in response to the rain

of catcalls and heavy gravel
   I needing to kill someone
  heaved a primeval rock

high across the back lane
   and into the very nest
  of the office typewriter

in the flat of Professor Sullivan
   who in the post-war years
  when he taught me calculus

amused the whole class
                    by retelling the tale
          after all it was not he

who had to bear
                    the lasting damage
          of that jangling chord from the struck

keys I could never
                    replicate on this machine
          What I am talking about

I lack
                    therefore I am
          however childish and

imperfectly remembered
                    is ontological
          has to do with the rare times

one trembles in bed
                    from terror
          out of love

one will completely dissolve
                    into this other person
          or when looking for encouragement

to the familiar
                    repetitions of the stars
          one recognizes

whatever that noble movement
                    you and I are not designed
          for this world we now live in

III.iii

Still less that first lake
                my grandfather's near Ste. Agathe
        so primeval it had no name

no road to the clearing
                and tree-trunk we used as a dock
        where Elizabeth and I

used to run naked
                among the spruce stumps
        or wade in the deep ooze

among the water lilies
                and murderous pitcher plants
        on the rotting logs

which ringed the lake
                bubbles of methane
        from soft things under our toes

We washed in water from a rain-barrel
                at a corner of the cabin
        pitched among boulders

where M. Desjardins
                watched his Guernseys even
        plowed a few desperate furrows

None of us belonged there
                not even the white horse
        we could not find the site of the farmhouse

when I went back with Selma
                snuck up the back way
        through Anson McKim's

and after a few hours
            the first rainstorm of that summer
      extinguished our hissing fire

my hopes of belonging
            to the pre-Cambrian north
      No! If I am to use language

then Lake Massawippi
            the one lake
      I could come back to

is the one we must deal with

                    III.iv

A poem of water
            why not the mountains
      the freedom on summits

to come down any side
            even the familiar one
      these afternoons I

walk up past the Rad Lab
            to look west from Grizzly Peak
      above the dim mists

in the skyscrapers
            the boats going nowhere
      and with dusk the first urgent

flashes of the signal
            taking over the night
      from uninhabited Alcatraz

just as when we had moved
                partly for my sake
        to Westmount Mountain

to go to school with kids
                who unaffectedly
        bore the names of firms

Birks Jewellers or Frosst's
                Neo-Chemical Food
        while the neighbor we never knew

except from the newspapers
                owned the Timmins gold mine
        yes then I felt liberated

looking out from Summit Circle
                where there were no fights
        over the city spread like a map

the Sun Life Building in the fog
                the dull murmur of the rapids
        the grainboats frozen in the canal

Under my mother's paintings
                and my father's piano
        I looked alone through the encyclopaedia

checking our family tree
                which my father pulled
        from a dusky trunk behind the furnace

futilely against the dukes
                and earls listed by name
        and date and little else

and in the warmth of spring
                I would go out before breakfast
        to look for the first bloodroots

in the park across the street
        or later that once
    our own white bodies

or just to play baseball
        with these children I called friends
    and when the black taxi

passed us and then stopped
        its passenger lay down in the street
    the soles of his shoes sticking up

and someone put a sheet
        over the rest of him
    I looked for it in the newspaper

and there were I believe instead
        the first headlines in my memory
    CHAMBERLAIN FLIES TO MUNICH

and the PEACE IN OUR TIME
        for which I woke up my parents
    to my embarrassment

I am losing the thread
        but yes it was that winter
    I sat up all night

by the window I was not supposed to close
        to face off the ghost of snow
    on the side of the oak tree

coming down as it seemed
        straight into my bedroom
    and could not turn away

or go back to the head of my bed
        until it faded in the dawn
    I still go to the high mountains

that rush of safe giddiness
        when I stand up and look around
    at so much visibility

flight
        immersion
        No! If we are to escape

we must go another way

                III.v

That bright island of non-being
        when I was eleven
        in Cambridge Massachusetts

as much of an escape
        into an exotic civilization
        as were those summers

near Ste. Agathe to something
        else I never was
        playing for the first time

with other sons of professors
        the son of a World Court judge
        the poet George Barker

as he was coming downstairs
        drinking the orange juice
        off my father's breakfast tray

and it was too much for our maid Georgette
        left speechless hands stretched
        across the alcove

transported too far
          from her native village in the Beauce
     Je suis la croix blanche   *I am the white cross*

vous m'avez rempli   *you have filled me*
          de forces électriques but I   *with electric current*
     for myself was glad to have

arrived among children who did not
          drag each other fully clothed
     into the gym shower glad

to trade Willkie buttons and debate
          in our small absolute way
     the need to get into the war

as Canada already had and whether
          I too should sing in the chorale
     the words about *bad King George*

glad not to be the first
          to be rebuked by Miss Thorp
     the grand-daughter of Longfellow

for being too rambunctious
          after school though next year
     I was less fit than before

to survive Westmount
          Junior High School among
     the draft dodgers who jammed Donald

from the Weirdale Orphanage
          accused of stealing pencils
     into the classroom waste-paper basket

such an easy mark that soon
          he quit school joined the Navy
     and was blown up by a sub in the St. Lawrence

I have to say that I myself once started
                that weekly joke *It's Donald's birthday*
        as if that might deflect the storm

Those years I mostly waited for the summers
                yet even now in North Hatley
        back among the Americans

I was either too snobbish or too uncouth
                either from uncompetitiveness
        or natural contrariety of mind

for that long season of
                canoeing and freestyle races
        the parents lined up on the dock at the Club

drinks in their hands and cheering
                Surely there must be
        some other way to grow up

I used to think with the water
                of the winners' kicks in my face
        or at the hour

of the confident male laughter
                from the six p.m. sherry parties
        I would rather listen to

from far up
                in the silent beech forest
        where I had gone back sullenly

to look for lady's slippers
                and found once deep in leaves
        three blue and brown speckled eggs

of what must have been
an ovenbird's nest

III.vi

Soon I would sail away
            through the ice storms of the North Atlantic
      as if to be born

with the leather briefcase
            I would use for a quarter century
      Betty Ann gave me the day

I said to her *thank you*
            and now good-bye
      after two righteous years

of the McGill Choral Society
            of McGill Outing Club hikes
      with their roughly innocent overnights

and of rallies of support
            against police brutality
      having seen

the glint of horses' hooves
            in the dark foreign-speaking crowds
      on the sidewalks of St. Lawrence Main

the pushing so determined
            on both sides of the Iron Curtain
      to establish the post-war era

with so much intrigue
            the result was complicity
      as in a small way

even I discovered
            the night five of us
      two friends one fellow-traveller one CP   *Communist Party*

roneoed the leaflets   *mimeoed*
      for an illegal march
   against the ban on marches

sworn to secrecy that night
      a blinding five a.m. rain
   we never handed the leaflets out

but the police came anyway
      first plain-clothes and then Mounties
   finally drawing a big crowd

enough for page three of the *Gazette*
      there being more than meets the eye
   to the politics of reason

and I do not know to this day
      whether one of us was an informant
   and whether even he

knew which side
      he was really working for
   nor to what extent

his wishes
could be distinguished from my own

III.vii

I arrived in no mood
      for the obligatory pluralism
   of post-war Oxford

where in our seminar
      on *Recent European*
   Political Thought

we were persuaded to read three dons
               from the south side of Broad Street
          and three from the north

my suggestion of Sartre
               meeting with a look which convinced
          even me I had just been joking

But where the theatrics of the gown
               turned Wordsworth back
          on his inner tranquility

they left me self-conscious
               the more insecure
          alone on Snowdon —

straddling a hog's back
               my giddiness
          in the dense fog

like a rodeo rider
               but in the end the sunburst
          over the summit revealed

no more than a cog railway
               sloping down into the west
          Then I discovered Hegel

sweet dialectics — now I knew
               the *world* was *an sich*
          and *I* was *für sich* the

no reality without accident
               which so annoyed the famous don
          if Hegel wrote that he shouldn't have

and even my kindly
               All Souls tutor
          whom I did not know

had himself been ploughed
        said of my mock-writtens
    they'll think you're insane

that was it — when Sally
        who had surprised me with a kiss
    on the canal towpath

outside Long Wittenham
        came to my digs for tea
    I tripped over the electric fire

branding the Astrakhan carpet
        of Mrs. Foxley-Norris
    and the only solution

stared up at me
        out of the mystic
    cipher at my feet

I was going mad
        the world even the war
    in Korea forgotten

for the momentary solace
        of incapacity
    body and fingers stretched

and I hear again my voice
        failing to reach me
    remember the long search

under moaning walnut-trees
        in the night rain near Limoges
    high wind off the Atlantic

to find any shelter
        one leg over the high
    courtyard wall when suddenly

the mastiff leapt up
        to the limit of its chain
     no sleep after that

and the next afternoon
        over the Puy-de-Sancy
     blocked by new snow from arriving

for Easter mass in the remote
        church of Orcival
     I swear I see

beyond the humming phone wire
        and glistening black asphalt
     a face in the heavy clouds

or was it
        in the strange light
     an intimation

of those shapes in the brooding
        toils of energy
     and deluge of emotion

we all carry within us

III.viii

As predicted the famous don
        frustratingly sympathetic
     said *but your Hegel questions*

sounded almost like Michael Foster
        and I thought back
     to the tea and crumpets

in the ill-lit immense
            study at Christ Church
     with the one don I found

not just a friend but in some ways
            a holy man as if
      in the wrong place and age

so there was no extra year
            as editor of the *Isis*
     it was back to Canada

and a small school
            for the over-privileged
      in the woods of the Seignory Club

where at night I read
            about Yvain in the forest
com hon forsenez et sauvage   *like a man frantic and wild*
                                                              Yvain 2838

but after the weekly movies
            the whole school cheering
      the gooks on Okinawa

once more incinerated
            in the jets of napalm spewed
      from the tanks of the Marines

lights out the generator switched off
            I would go out in the moonlight
      boots squeaking on snow

to empty the steadily filling
            buckets of maple sap
      into the boys' vats

and stoke their banked fires
            the woods' shadows numinous
      with sugary smoke

and I have since believed
        in the face of
    every nuclear headline

the force flooding those
            millions of high trees
    even in the frost of night

will survive the next war
            whether or not we do
    and I found I had the courage

to make my young warriors
            read one account
    of an actual lynching

jabbering foaming at the mouth
            horrible white of his eyes   Davies 141
    till they begged me to stop

to say it didn't happen
            now that was a discovery
    Three years later I went back

on my honeymoon with Maylie
            to that tall carpeted room
    over Christ Church Meadow

asking in effect
            from this same new-found power
    How can you stand it here?

And Michael Foster a few months
            before he shot himself
    looked around at the oak

panels from Cardinal Wolsey
            and said *I can't imagine*
    any better life

78

III.ix

With the same remoteness
          or if you will emancipation
     by which I managed

to be ploughed at Oxford   *failed*
          I went on for three years
     without falling in love

and for what then seemed tragic
          I can have no regrets
     there is something to be said

for being marginal
          and even insular
     at the vortices of culture

like Oxford and Harvard
          where the sons of the wealthy
     at their Eliot House breakfasts

ate only the yolks of their eggs
          Certainly I was glad
     to have been drafted neither

for Kenya nor Korea
          neither the black-tie dinners
     of my Rhodes Scholar roommates

nor the emphatic
          intellectual summitry
     of the Harvard Junior Fellows

all chosen for high careers
          If we were large-minded enough
     and could plough everyone

send them back to the forests
            like Yvain or Erlangga
        like the heroes of all good tales

then no one would have
            needed to look shocked
        that night in New York

when in the company of
            my friends the Rhodes Scholars
        and Junior Fellows

gearing up to publish
            their policy dissertations
        to burst upon the world

of think-tanks the CFR
            and consulting for agencies
        as yet unnamed

I said *That's why*
            some people in Europe
        are not so upset

to see Russia get the bomb
            and you could hear the drinks
        of the future ambassadors

being set down

III.x

The stream one lives by
        one hardly hears
    we are not astronauts

who see today's light
               as a disc of radiance
          inhabiting darkness

and to that reader
               who like myself has been plunged
          to the heart of once terrifying

now daily love
               it will be clear why these words
          cast no dark shadows

though there was once such a dawn
               the word *love* itself decays
          till it loses meaning

and now that to think
               of escape is meaningless
          and one feels free

even to scream rather than escape
               indeed could one ever scream
          this way at God I wonder

how exonerate her
               for the criminal defects
          of the whole establishment

including life itself
               she first delivered me from
          unlike everyone else

even my dear father and mother
               whose saving dissatisfactions
          I look back on as defined

even my own children
               issuing forward
          like the new energy

spilling from clefts in the ocean bed
        you will not see her
     anywhere in this poem

except as one sees light
        as in the darkness
     floating between my thigh

and my quiet fingers
        she may seem no more than a
     rest within space

no more than a
        pivot
     for the restless movements of the stars

she being within the
        crannies of what is written
     beyond what it limits

and when she sleeps

III.xi

After my father's biographer
        has visited I have
     this dream of sitting

beside the door of our house
        from which bodies are being
     removed it becomes

more and more clear there is
        some kind of major scandal
     though the house is mine now

I am not aware of
             terror even guilt
        it is more like the discovery

of Philip of Macedon's tomb
             in museum photographs
        the tunnel having been dug

through generations of suppressed
             memory by the biographer
        how my great–great–grandfather

John Scott came to Montreal
             on one of the cholera ships
        to open a stationery shop

and died soon after
             as did his eldest son
        leaving young William Edward

to support the whole family
             as apothecary's apprentice
        and eventually doctor

five of whose nine children
             died by the age of four
        of the family consumption

Djwa 14-15

my grandfather Frederick George
             the first not suckled
        by his mother and also

the first to survive — a poet
             and young Anglo–Catholic curate
        who drawn to a monastery

when his sister parents
             and beloved died
        wrote *when Death comes*

Sin sits and hums
            A chaunt of fears
my grandfather the jovial

Beloved Padre who walked
            into No Man's Land
            on all sides the brown mud   *F.G. Scott 156-57*

and desolate mist till he saw
            the hand of my Uncle Harry
with the Scott family ring   *Djwa 38*

the bloodstone fake crest I wear myself
            on the little finger
Uncle Arthur too the prize-winning

debater in high school
            who never spoke again in public
            I could feel my legs paralyzed

as if turning to stone
            and became a notary
            and yet my father the thirties pacifist

his four older brothers
            all dead or badly wounded
was only prevented from enlisting

at seventeen by the rifle
            which exploded in his hands
and blew out one eye

life after that
            so concentrated in his tingling limbs
he became like his own father

poet reformer domestic tyrant
            the father whom as a child
he had avoided sick in bed

84

I see my father in the dying man
            and straight toward me
      endless the known and unknown roadways run   *F.R. Scott 169*

it is all coming out
            the funeral I must have forgotten
      Dick Scott

torpedoed in the St. Lawrence
            I have not escaped death's nudge
      they are emerging now

from the house of my dream
            the dead
      and the survivors

the fallen apples of the dead
            beyond ourselves
      the yet untasted

tree of life

                    III.xii

After the ritual
            procession to the sea
      and the empty beach with its spirits

a cockfight much feasting   *Belo 99*
            the shadows gather
      of the village ancestors

in the *wajang koelit*
            the shadow play
      adapted to centuries

of invading powers
        now no more than fragments
    of the original story

the Barata Yudda or great war
        delighting its audience
    less with its five heroes

the virtuous Pendawas
        of Hindu origin
    aloof esoteric Arjuna

the too *perfectly just*   *Geertz '73 139*
        banished to the forest
    than with the heroes' servants

the clown Toealen
        true Indonesian ancestor
    black pot-bellied

permanently pregnant   *de Zoete 156*
        who by his crafty
    knowledge of the occult

makes his hero appear
        always to be conqueror   *Covarrubias 241*
    or the clown Semar

Falstaffian jester
        who when the too dutiful
    Arjuna under orders

comes to execute him
        replies *old friend*
    I will burn myself

in the fire rising
        to defeat Shiva
    so the war starts again   *Geertz '73 139-40*

Visitors cannot understand
            how the great crowds
       can go on watching till dawn

or in the case
            of the *tjalonarang*
       the powerful exorcism

how after a day's work
            the village dancers
       go so easily into trance

to *bring the gods down*
            not that this will
       have anything to do with

the rising birth rate
            or the shortage of land
       but the anger they rarely show

fires the combat
            between the terrible witch Rangda
       her long hanging breasts

realistically made
            of bags of white cloth
       filled with sawdust   *Covarrubias 326*

not only a fear-inspiring figure
            she is Fear
       afraid as well as frightening   *Bateson and Mead 35-36*

whose deathly plague has
            destroyed the kingdom
       of her son Erlangga

and the good dragon Barong
            whose sheepdog coat
       glitters with mica

moving among the kris dancers
        entranced by Rangda
    to return them to consciousness

gentle Balinese father
        according to Bateson and Mead
    a frenzied trancer

has only to rub his face
        in the Dragon's beard
    to be calmed   *Bateson and Mead 38*

even Rangda who may run amok
        headlong into the *gamelan*   *orchestra*
    or be deranged for weeks

has her comic moments
        as when she pretends to polish
    the mirrors on Barong's coat

while members of the crowd
        in trance around the courtyard
    rush out to stab themselves

wrestle with one another
        devour live chicks or excrement
    as the spectators

relieve them of their krisses
        because those not fully
    estranged can wound themselves

until towards dawn
        the actor possessed
    by the real Rangda

is brought with effort under control
        one old actor is said
    never to have regained

his mental balance   *Covarrubias 331*
        and the great battle is
    once more a standoff

                    III.xiii

It was after I looked up
        C.F. Adams of Pan Am
    because of Air America and

the CIA's phony Laos crisis
        of 1959   *P.D. Scott '72 10-15*
        that I found out I knew

not one but two Adamses
        Gill the sophomore
    who dropped out of Radcliffe

to live in the Berkshires
        singing madrigals
    and whose father (through

Paul Mellon's Bollingen Foundation)
        published the books
        I was then reading

by Curtius and Auerbach
        on imperial pastorals
    parola ornata   *Curtius 71, 357*

ascent from the depths   *Curtius 6*
        and forest romances
    commissioned by the wives

of absent crusaders
        dir soave e piana   *Auerbach 66*
    which even if Europe

                        89

should now lose its power
　　　　has prefigured a common life　　　　　　*Auerbach 338*
　　and the other Adams

George Homans president
　　　　of the American Sociological Association
　　who went so quickly down the lake

to fetch my father
　　　　from the camp on Black Point
　　when Maylie went into hospital

and who wrote about rank
　　　　If his behavior had improved
　　his social rank might then have risen　　　　*Homans '50 180*

no one had more verve
　　　　for those Hatley cocktails
　　but when my cousin Ibby

protested the napalmed
　　　　villages in Vietnam
　　George shouted at the surprised

Canadians *we will win*
　　　　we will win
　　George is it possible

I wonder speaking myself
　　　　as a refugee third-
　　generation Canadian poet

that we are all victims
　　　　of excessive inheritance
　　after all you yourself

apparently believed
　　　　every single bit
　　of human behavior

III.xiv

My mother walked out of that
                    Hatley get-together
          I never had the guts

to walk out of the
                    quadripartite
          disarmament talks at the UN

while Henry Cabot Lodge
                    in his impeccable
          Champs Elysées café French

was putting on another of his
                    affected or possibly sincere
          stupidity acts

thus forestalling
                    what was probably in any case
          the quite imaginary risk

of disarmament I
                    am not suggesting
          Valerian Zorin was any different

still less that the problem was
                    automatically one of caste
          Kent School's Jake Beam

having learnt to speak Polish
                    to President Zawadzki
          the former railway worker

with a good humor that
        disqualified him
    for the hard-edged nightmare

at the power center alas
        so many new nations
    so many ambitious men

still candidates for
        the curse of pre-eminence
    not yet terrorized by war

and now bloodbaths in peacetime
        they have designed for themselves
    with the insomniac clarity

one associates with mountains
        the roof of the world
    the long faces

in D.L.1   *Defense Liaison 1 (External Affairs)*
        when they heard the new Prime Minister
    had signed without thinking

the NORAD agreement
        slipped him as if routine   *Ignatieff 188-89*
    or even that private UN dinner

out on Long Island the
        Iranian host a Cypriot
    the Ethiopian princess whose uncle

died later in the coup
        and when my boss called me back
    for the meaningless midnight

vote in the UN First Committee
        it was mountain clear
    driving in on the freeway

at sixty miles an hour
            my life entrusted willingly
      to the unpromising

strangers on my right and left
            that the government of the world
      could be arranged like this

the problem not so much
            simple human incompetence
      or evil on all sides

but those unique degradations
            which follow upon any
      categorical assumption

of command

                  III.xv

The year
            I was consul in Warsaw
      hour after morning hour

I would tell the marriageable
            village princesses
      fatally decked out in their best

hand-embroidered *strój*   *folk dresses*
            who had risen at 2:30 a.m.
      to catch the milk train

that if they too
            wished to visit cousins
      in the mining towns

of flat northern Ontario
        for a six-week holiday
    then unlike their post-

menopausal mothers and aunts
        they would have to get x-rays
    and apply through Ottawa to become

landed immigrants I having taken
        only seconds to size up
    their nubility

and then deliver
        the disastrous verdict
    to certain tears and pleadings

which in turn came back
        in not necessarily unpleasant
    ways to haunt my dreams

No one should have to or be
        allowed to last in such a job
    the talent for power

being almost certainly
        a disqualification
    just as governments

that limit themselves
        with domestic restraints
    Athens Rome England even Spain

almost immediately
        in an unfilled world
    explode into empires   *Marshall '87 227*

like giant doomed stars

III.xvi

Strictly speaking
         the only multinational financier
    I ever knew was Raleigh

youngest child
         and gentlest father
    and if I remember him

once wearing a cutaway
         it was only as a joke
    on himself at a Halloween party

or perhaps when I was seven
         and married his daughter Elizabeth
    in a Lachute barn

no Marxist could have talked with Raleigh
         for one hour and still hated him
    and yet it was Raleigh

in his unsung job
         with an insignificant pension
    in the investment department

of the Sun Life Assurance Company
         Montreal's largest
    who dealt with Curtis Calder

of Havana Electric
         Shanghai Power Company
    and Italian Superpower

Raleigh who when we had tea
         in his small retirement apartment
    to talk about finance

had never heard
        of Meyer Lansky's racetrack
    leased to him by Citibank

where he corrupted
        the Cuban politicians or
    of Tu Yueh-Sheng's Green Gang

which Chiang and Tai Li
        used to wipe out the Shanghai
    Communists and run the dope traffic

Raleigh and his department
        who innocently
    as the Aswan engineers

not thinking about snails
        helped persuade
    a reluctant General Motors

to build a plant in South Africa
        so that the earnings
    from Sun Life's premiums

could be invested in place
        and not create pressure
    on the Krugerrand

In accordance with Plato
        he kept to his station
    as the best of us have done

III.xvii

The Radja had expected
        his palace to be attacked
    from the south side

as martial custom would require
        but unexpectedly
    the Dutch made for the north

his household
        in a collective frenzy
    half dazed with opium   *Geertz '80 11*

set the palace on fire
        all his relatives
    dressed in their white finest

with gold ceremonial krisses
        the women even more
    enthusiastic than the men

in short white loincloths
        covered with jewelry
    their hair loose

carrying spears broken in half
        to be used at close range
    The procession left the palace

with the Radja at its head
        on a man's shoulders and protected
    by his gold umbrellas of state

entranced women and boys
        marched up the avenue
    to the astonished Dutch

who gave orders to halt
        but they only walked faster
    then made an insane rush

the soldiers fired the first volley
        and a few fell but
    the frenzied men and women

continued to attack
        the soldiers to avoid
    being overrun were obliged

to fire continually
        someone with a kris
    went around killing the wounded

he was shot down but
        an old woman took the kris
    and continued the bloody task

the wives of the Radja
        stabbed themselves
    in a heap over his body

when the horrified soldiers
        stopped firing
    the women threw gold coins

yelling that it was payment
        for a final shot
    or else stabbed themselves

everywhere broken spears
        krisses with gold handles
    studded with diamonds and rubies

in pools of blood   *Covarrubias 34-35*

A woman survivor
        who fainted when cut
    by the spear of a falling man

told Covarrubias
        all she remembered was
    the cool hissing of the bullets

like music

Mégève   coming down
        beside a rainbow
    into a shower

glissade 1000 meters
        on wet grass
    laughter at falling safe

think   married a Venezuelan
            and lives near Lausanne
    tell me now you

with homes in the mountains
        who are at hand
    and know all things

where we hear only rumor
        of the captains
    at Bilderberg meetings

one has to sound
        like a John Bircher to talk about
    between the Rockefellers

the Agnellis and the Rothschilds
        at whose Mégève resort
    we were lodged in uncomfortable

luxury as delegates
        to the International Student Service
    Bilderberg meetings

supplying Prince Bernhard with
        an almost unrivalled network   *Doyle 20*
    not just for the European Movement

financed with German counterpart funds
  but also for the recruitment
 of old intelligence contacts

as conduits for Lockheed payoffs
  through the Temperate Zone
 Research Foundation

for Antelope Cobbler the Italian premier   *Sampson '77 135-36*
  which supplemented the CIA's
 financial support

to parties candidates
  and incumbent leaders
 of almost every political persuasion   *Church I,146*

and under Sukarno
  which is why I am telling all this —
 not just recalling

the swampy fields
  around the Rockefeller lodge
 in the Connecticut valley

where the Liberty Lobby discovered
  the Bilderbergers in '67 —
 Jakarta payments deflected

four months before the coup   *Sampson '77 184-85*
  at legal risks to Lockheed   *'76 Hearings 962*
 towards the *very wealthy*

General Alamsjah
  epitome of
 the military entrepreneur   *Crouch 243*

whom a Lockheed memo
  called *the second man*
 the coup made at once

funds available to Suharto   *'76 Hearings 962*
          a Lockheed web   *P.D. Scott '85A 256*
     extending from Geneva to Jakarta   *Sampson '77 120*

millions to Japanese officials
          where *every move made*
          was approved by Washington   *Sampson '77 228*

the money through Deak
          back to Shig Katayama
     in the Cayman Islands   *'75 Hearing 909*

the Wildlife Fund the Sultan
          Castle Bank in the Bahamas
     Helliwell narcotics CIA   *Kruger 15-16*

the name Richard M. Nixon on the list   *'75 Hearing 241*
          It was at a Bilderberg
     meeting that Prince Bernhard

was introduced by Baron
          Edmond de Rothschild
     to Tibor Rosenbaum of the ICB   *Doyle 20*

the International Credit Bank   *Naylor 22*
          (later exposed by the Baron
     after the Vesco coup

as *a source of secret funds*
          for the Mossad
     Israel's intelligence service

and one of the country's primary
          weapons brokers)   *Hougan 172*
     and whose colleague Ed Levinson

was the power behind
          the Havana Riviera   *Reid 226*
     and the Serv-U Corporation

of the Bobby Baker payoffs
        which began to be exposed
    in November 1963 —

My book would have asked
        as the Warren Commission staff
    working for Allen Dulles

was unable to
        why Levinson's pit-boss
    McWillie *gambler and murderer*   *23 WH 166*

from the old Binion gang
        in Dallas and Fort Worth
    who *had a fix with Mr. Big*

I don't think we'd better
        go into that phase of it   *Reid 156-57*
    twice brought to Havana

most likely as a courier   *AR 152*
        his close friend
    Jack Ruby

A dumb subject
        The book went into galleys
    and was photographed

for the Pocket Books spring catalogue
        but never published
    freeing me

to write this poem
        Do you remember   yes
    just for an instant

the sun warm on our shoulders
          and beyond the mists
      rising from the meadow

Mont Blanc

IV.ii

From the Bay Bridge
          on the way home from the opera
      you could look down on the searchlights

of the Oakland Army Terminal
          where they loaded the containers
      of pellet-bombs and napalm

into black Japanese ships
          over which the cranes
      bent like anxious surgeons

in the calm and glassy night
          People of good will
      of whom at first there were many

were willing to sign petitions   *Powers 36*
          or to help in drafting
      the letter to the *Times*

about how in six months
          they had moved from true to false
      reports of the North Vietnamese

negotiating position   *Schurmann '66 92-93*
          that letter never published
      and the music changing

bonfires to still the streets
        the first smudges of tear gas
    the Yellow Submarine

(acid in Big Sur
        Allen kneeling to pray
    for Johnson's health)

at the rock poetry festival
        no sensations from my first joint
    except for the difference

between the salt and pepper
        I felt being shaken
    on my bare left arm

Owsley by parachute
        at the Human Be-in
    Mika on Carole's shoulders

on mine so they could see
        the Brave New World
    worms in the rose   *Lee 162*

the party's hostess
        some new drug in the basement
    crying like a child

CIA personnel
        helping local chemists
    set up LSD labs

in the Bay Area
        to monitor events   *Lee 188-89*
    STP Serenity

from Dow Chemical
        and the Edgewood Arsenal
    like being shot out of a gun   *Lee 187*

men with their Sunday morning
        rifle range target practice
   Black Panthers Ku Klux Klan

women who shyly hinted
        at ineffable orgies
of acid nakedness

Ed Sanders the Fugs
       investigative poetics
Out demons out

with *no respect whatsoever*
      for the unassailable logic
of the next step   *Mailer 86*

two hundred pounds of daisies
        from Peggy Hitchcock
to skybomb the Pentagon

Fort Funston Beach
       the Barb's first nude-in
under the fixed gaze of the mounted police

dunes of iceplant and callas
       linnets in the sun and mist
   (*To shoot a policeman*

is a sacred act)   *Lee 265*
       the women in seaweed and surf
  wading as if to be washed

as clean as seals

There must be two of me
        I remember the surge
   of almost too vivid pleasure

when the sheriffs lined up
        their faces and numbers masked
   the streetlights' reflections

caught in the burnish
        of their identical helmets
   and we found we could hold our terrain

the smoking canisters
        of tear gas hurled back
   there were so many more of us

or to watch the incompetent
        Vice-President of Buildings
   who had never once met

anyone who could explain
        why his blueprints for Peoples' Park
   were denounced as murderous

he being as determined
        to maintain what he called order
   as the tribes to upheave it

the difference not always clear
        and when the helicopter
   darkened half the sky

with CS gas
        I myself wanted to reach
   for a machine-gun but

when the clenched fists went off
        down Telegraph towards
    the waiting fence

the canisters popping
        like white fourth of July rockets
    and the sheriffs loading their rifles

with .303 buckshot
        the moment everyone had been waiting for
    for someone James Rector to get killed

I watched from the second-story window
        of Wheeler Hall with John
    the middle-aged mafia contractor

boyfriend of my teaching assistant
        who had told her
    the night Bobby Kennedy was shot

our boys must have done it
        and whom the U.S. Government
    had flown to Saigon

to handle the waterfront corruption
        Through the thick glass and
    oak frame of the dormer window

we watched the meridional blue sky
        with so much white gas in it
    above the plane trees

which later sickened
        and wept their leaves
    and I said to him *John*

which was not his name *don't worry*
        I'm sure Karen is in the library
    she wouldn't be out there

and never said until this sentence
        the whiteness
    of those distraught mafia knuckles

is what I
        still carry with me
    from this supposedly historic day

IV.iv

When after the dinners
        in the expensive East Side restaurants
    I used to go back

to the Mission code machines
        speeding my dictated reports
    to Ottawa that night

with copies to Washington
        London Paris for possible
    sharing with *our* NATO *allies*

not a word I wrote then
        was worth being recorded
    let alone labeled TOP SECRET

Later reading declassified
        copies of the U.S. traffic
    of those years

I felt outside the dimensions
        of the flattened bureaucratese
    that once seemed normal

COMMIES KORCOMS CHICOMS   *Korean, Chinese Communists*
        from people in the State Department
    not really witting of course

but anxious to prove
        they were on the team
    if we are prepared abandon

hope influencing Sukarno
        and if we still believe army
    best bet to keep INDO

out of COMMIE *hands* etc.
        if we can give them
    this kind of shot in arm

they might have more inclination act   *DD '75 120D 1/9/65*
        Or in the very month
    of *Time* Magazine's disclosure

the disposal of the corpses
        has created a serious sanitation problem
    small rivers and streams

have been literally clogged with bodies
        river transportation
    has at places been impeded   *Time 12/17/65*

emotion without judgment
        as if *pour encourager les autres*
    while the language of world order

is one of judgment
        at any cost
    uncontaminated by emotion

e.g. *military leaders' campaign*
        to destroy PKI
    is moving swiftly and smoothly

(an outgoing from George Ball
        the opponent of escalation
    and *devil's advocate* i.e. the one lone dove)

we may be confronted within weeks
with situation we have hoped for
i.e. a new government   *DD '76 83G 12/16/65*

or this incoming from the new Ambassador
elimination continues apace
party formally terminated

in fourteen provinces
only eleven more to go!
continuing massacre Bali

many headless bodies
encountered on roads
tourists well advised

to postpone pleasure trips
to island of the gods   *DD '76 84A 12/20/65*
A society which

declassifies its documents
after it is too late
to make any difference

will publish anything
as did the *L.A. Times* —
The Communist Party

attempted to seize power
and subjected the country   *L.A. Times 11/15/75*
to a national bloodbath   *Chomsky 216*

Or you Robert Shaplen
writing from CIA sources
for *The New Yorker*

They went to their deaths
in white funeral robes
with an astonishing passivity

as if admitting their guilt   Shaplen 123-24

IV.v

Action! I do not mean
            the log bouncing four times
    down from the jackladder

into the Rivière aux Outardes
            the fluke by which I survived
    the stinking bunkhouse

of the Quebec North Shore Paper Company
            with men who could spend
    six weeks salary on a Rimouski weekend

even less the compromise
            Canadian amendment
    which to the distress of the French

passed by a large majority
            at the Conference on Diplomatic Intercourse
    in the grand hall of the Vienna Hofburg

I mean the melancholy beauty
            of a fog-calm morning
    on the Sproul Hall steps

which Governor Reagan
            had declared off-limits
    to any assembly

between a few chilly spectators
                and the gas-masked
        riot-helmeted highway patrol

we were thirty faculty
                asserting a high view
        of our constitutional rights

and when the patrolmen
                arms linked billy-clubs
        presented but not menacing

began to push us
                so silently you could still hear
        the baffled pigeons

the fountain in the wet gloom
                they came first to myself
        and to David Krech

who had already suffered
                his first bad heart attack
        I looked in his face

forgetting all the others
                as if to say *Krech*
        what does one do now

they are moving so slowly
                that if we somehow
        refuse to be displaced

we will have converted
                history into that moment
        of resolution

all of us have been waiting
                so many years for
        but it was too late

already we were
              being nudged to one side
        in slow motion

the way a sure hand guides
              crumbs off a table
        to where the captain

in the presence of all of us
              said *congratulations*
        for a job well done

but we all knew there
              is no easier task
        than to sweep away faculty

it was not in the next day's paper
              not even the campus paper
        and I knew afterwards

the failure was not just
              our lack of planned options
        but my much older habit

of inevitably looking
              to someone else
        and though Krech is now

dead I still think of
              that moment face turned
        impending sticks helmets

those baffled eyes

He who sits mind brooding
             over his self-restraint
      is called a hypocrite said Krishna   *Bhag. Gita* 3.6

or as Mailer observed
             at the steps of the Pentagon
      it was *a large blemish*

that they were supine
             like a string of fish   *Mailer 276-77*
      the left calling Martin Luther

King an Uncle Tom
             but Sir Winston Churchill
      found it *alarming*

and also nauseating to see
             the Viceroy summon
      a seditious Middle Temple lawyer

now posing as a fakir
             of a type well-known in the East
      striding half-naked up the steps

of the Viceregal palace   *Payne 404*
             Gandhi first met the Gita
      in the Sir Edwin Arnold translation

through the London Vegetarian Society
             and Madame Blavatsky's theosophists
      but what to Churchill seemed inauthentic

and to Indians unscholarly
             the Pandavas had exhausted all avenues
      the war was actually forced on them

it would be unbecoming of Arjuna
        as a hero and ksatriya   *warrior*
    to refuse to fight   *Betai 239, 237*

is just what makes Gandhi
        more than his roots
    as when for his acceptance

of voluntary fingerprinting
        he was felled *he Rama* with a cudgel   *O God*
    kicked and beaten in his blood

by a Pathan Mir Alam   *Payne 181*
        who would later apologize
    with a warm handclasp   *Erikson 204*

at the Hamidia mosque
        as the Johannesberg Indians
    burned their registration certificates

and he sustained himself in jail
        on Thoreau a life of Garibaldi
    and the Koran

and when he translated
        Ruskin's *Unto This Last*
    into his native Gujarati

it was as a text
        for Tolstoy Farm in the Transvaal
    and later the Sabarmati ashram

the first *fasting for light*   *Payne 441*
        was to force not the British
    but the leaders of the Depressed Classes

to rescind their demands
        for a separate electorate
    I would far rather

that Hinduism died
>> *than that untouchability lived*   *Payne 439*
> and the last was to force

the new Indian cabinet
>> to reverse itself
> and pay the new state of Pakistan

its share of the old divided treasury
>> shunning the London Conference
> he trekked through the Muslim

villages of Noakhali
>> where thousands of Hindus
> had been killed or forcibly converted

to hold prayer meetings
>> once even in a mosque
> and gradually restore peace

Gandhi wrote to a friend
>> *truth and nonviolence have sustained me*
> *for the last sixty years*

but today I seem to miss
>> *the certainty of that power*   *Kytle 173*
> and when he was *he Rama* murdered   *O God*

the new government
>> needing to honor him
> gave him a military funeral

transported his body
>> on a flower-bedecked
> weapons carrier

while overhead Dakotas
        of the Royal Indian Air Force
    dipped in salute

with *showers of scented blossoms*   *Kytle 182*

IV.vii

On the night train to Kraków
        the Polish engineers
    among the ficelles of vegetables

and the smell of the peasants' tobacco
        would talk excitedly
    about the prospects for extracting sulphur

from great depths or the problem
        of feeding the cities now that
    the peasants had taken back

their family half-hectare plots
        (here they lowered their voices)
    and would not buy tractors

believing like ourselves
        in the *philosophy of growth*
    with its propensity to distance

the planners ever more from the people
        the barefoot goat-herd girl near Warsaw
    in the Breughel landscape

we beheld from the Vistula dike
        from the Leninist auto-critique
    published in Prague

suicidal leftist policies
         the Chinese comrades
    not averse to capitalizing   Mrázek 164-65

to which the Czech student
         of Professor Anderson
    added *No American*

could claim that U.S. training
         had strengthened Suharto   Mrázek 172
    who *tried to unify*

under the spirit of jago-satria   *fighting-cock, warrior*
         and was spared by the commandos
    because he was *not corrupted*

and *westernized*   Mrázek 184, 171
         It has been said many times
    but only by the powerless

wherever the quality of work
         is a function of productivity
    and not vice versa

(I will say it again)
         the growth of society
    towards maximized product

is accompanied by the enslavement of the subject

                          IV.viii

Clifford Geertz having just
         reread your *Notes*
    on the Balinese cockfight

how you were first accepted
        by the cautious villagers
    after you all fled

from the Javanese constabulary
        and how slaughter
    in the cock ring itself

after *red pepper*
        is stuffed down their beaks
    and up their anuses   *Geertz '73 419*

joins *pride to selfhood*
        selfhood to cocks
    and cocks to destruction   *Geertz '73 444*

a blood sacrifice
        offered to the demons
    to pacify their cannibal hunger   *Geertz '73 420*

depicting how things are among men
        not literally but almost worse
    imaginatively

what it says is
        it is of these emotions
    that society is built   *Geertz '73 449*

and of the combat
        between the terrible witch Rangda
    her eyes bulging like boils

and the endearing monster Barong
        a clash between the malignant
    and the ridiculous   *Geertz '73 114*

It is not your belief that men
        every last one of them are cultural artifacts   *Geertz '73 51*
    that I now question

or even that *the imposition*
　　　of meaning on life
　　　is the major end of human existence　　　　　　*Geertz '73 434*

that Virgilian flourish
　　　in your footnote to Max Weber
　　　but your recurring interpretations

of the Balinese massacre
　　　after what you choose to call
　　　the bungled coup and its savage aftermath　　　　*Geertz '73 322*

My complaint is not
　　　of your early field project
　　　for Ford and the CIA-funded

Center at MIT
　　　in which you preceded Pauker
　　　or your commissioned study

on which local elites
　　　would best play a role
　　　in Rostow's *pre-take-off period*　　　　　　*Geertz '63 3*

I will not cast that stone
　　　from this front window
　　　of the world's largest weapons lab

you who know about
　　　puputan and *Tjalonarang*　　　*ritual suicide, trance drama*
　　　have the right to recall

the fact of *the massacre*
　　　through the medium of the *cockfight*
　　　the theatricality of trance　　　　　　*Geertz '73 452*

but why did you write
　　　several hundred thousand
　　　people were massacred

120

largely villagers by other villagers
  though there were some
army executions as well   *Geertz '73 282*

when even Shaplen admits
    the murders in Bali
did not start until early December   *Shaplen 124*

that is until after
    Colonel Edhie's commandos
with unit-names like *Dracula*

had finished in East Java   *P.D. Scott '85A 244*
    the army began it
then handed the job over to the Balinese   *Shaplen 125*

that is to the *special teams*
    set up under Nasution's
and Suharto's orders   *May 123*

and finally stopped the bloodletting
    as the smell of burning houses
overpowered the customary

fragrance of the rich island flora   *Shaplen 125*
    Clifford Geertz sometimes
the world is not as mysterious

as you and I might wish
    why can you not write
as straightforwardly as *Time*   *Time 12/17/65*

about the land to which you returned
    on a junta visa
and how can you write

about *the integrative revolution*
    in a book that is indexed
to sixty-one countries

Paraguay the Soviet Union
but not the United States?

IV.ix

When some toys from the West
              were stolen out of the back seat
        of our Peugeot in Saska Kępa

I went without thinking
              to the Warsaw police
        A moustached officer

wrote down everything
              I had to say
        which was very little

and then asked me
              Was the door locked?
        I said I had no idea

probably not and he said
              Proszę Pana excuse me
        but it would be good in future

to keep your doors locked
              Our children are not used
        to seeing toys from the west

and you do not want
              to encourage them in crime
        those Sunday walks with

Cassie in her blue pram
              the well-dressed housewives
        offering in illegal dollars

twice what we had paid for it
        I told the officer
        I was withdrawing my complaint

He smiled and began to talk
        about his life as a policeman
        how much easier it had been

after Stalin had died
        In those days no one
        wanted to talk to us

even our own children
        sometimes mistrusting us
        despite what they learned at school

We talked for two hours
        and I think of him often
        as I read in the papers

of Solidarność suppressed
        how those must be
        privileged moments

one can so transcend history
        how today he would not dare
        to have such a conversation

nor I have the heart
        And yet those two hours
        in that ill-furnished precinct

seem somehow more true
        than the street battles since
        My own life is easier

no longer having to be consul
        I suspect that on our side
        officials of U.S. Steel

would find life easier
        not having to worry
    about what their children

were learning at university
        if they knew their smokestacks
    in Gary Indiana

did not threaten to kill off
        the salmon of Labrador
    and silence the weird laughter

of the loons

                    IV.x

The first coup
        after the fall of Kennedy and Minh
    was in Brazil

the highways pushed into the jungle
        big money
    for men like ▮▮▮▮▮ ▮▮▮▮▮▮

with CIA connections
        and the end of the Kaingang tribe
    feuds spread cleaving the society

wrote Jules Henry
        When Yakva says to me
    My cousin wants to kill me

I know he wants to kill his cousin
        who slaughtered his pigs
    for rooting up his corn   *Girard 52, 54*

but since then we have seen
        the corpses at Jonestown
    professors developing

subtle technologies
        for repression of protest
    and acceleration of the race

to nuclear suicide
        making Dan ask
    are we not Jonestown?

And what if the choices
        in Java were just
    as simple — to become

a technological graveyard
        stomachs torn open
    corpses deliberately impaled

on bamboo stakes   Kartawidjaja 44
        or a Malthusian one
    rice production beginning

to give way to high-yield
        low-nutrition cassava
    till petty landlords

rid themselves of peasants
        who had taken over the fields
    to enforce the government's

ineffectual land reform   Shaplen 121
        No! despite such choices
    it is clear we must resist

the black-shirted gangs
        some of whose own members
    experienced *recurring nightmares*

in which their victims appeared
　　　　before them like Banquo's ghost
　　and sought solace from doctors　　　　　　　　　　　*May 125*

like Wordsworth *enflamed with hope*
　　　　at the square of the Carousel
　　a *few weeks back*

heaped up with dead and dying
　　　　until he seemed to hear
　　a ghost *that cried to the*

whole city Sleep no more　　　　　　　　　　　*Prelude 10.38-77*
　　　　and those deaths Pauker imagined
　　no mere guilty memories

but portents

IV. xi

There is drought in the west
　　　　I have just flown east for a weekend
　　swum at my father's camp

and now dry myself in the
　　　　mist among the wet
　　red and yellow maple leaves

the lake so full the
　　　　beach is flooded and we
　　have to drop an anchor

from the boat's stern
　　　　but the big news
　　dividing the whole village

even my father from my mother
          is the Arab Gabr
    married to a Saudi princess

who wants to build
          an electronics factory
    on the other side of the lake

to train planeloads of Saudis
          brought over from Riyadh
    My father tells me

he can hardly afford the boat
          since the Arab bought up both marinas
    Ride's boathouse is

an office building with
          moslem arches in front
    my mother tells me

the French-Canadian shopkeepers
          need more business
    especially in winter

he wants to build here
          because he loves the lake so much
    there is no water in Arabia

Arbitrage! to save the dollar
          by monetizing oil   *Naylor 48-50*
    arms sales to the Shah

and I thought of Adnan Khashoggi
          the Indonesian shipping magnate
    Saudi friend of Pak

Chung Hee and Roy Furmark
          $106 million
    in Lockheed commissions

to *Khashoggi alone*   *Sampson '77 275*
      and twice that
      amount withdrawn by Khashoggi

from Rebozo's bank in Key Biscayne
      in May and November '72   *Adler 93*
      and of Lim Suharto's *cukong*   *Chinese partner*

who has bought the Hibernia bank
      with a branch on the Berkeley campus
      from profits on arms deals

handled by the New York lawyer
      whose wife helped liberal causes (including mine)
      some kind of storm brewing   *May 224-27*

And I thought of the Arab in Wordsworth's dream
      a loud prophetic
      blast of harmony   *Prelude 5.96*

portending deluge

IV. xii

Is this not a lesson for you
      designers of policy
      who have been carefully trained

to ignore your instincts
      except that of surpassing
      You would not be so foolish

as to seek health through weight
      yet having sought growth
      through economic expansion

you now seek security
       through aggrandisement
   not even for commerce

at which others now exceed us
       but for the enforcement
   of miserable debt

Only our belief in strength
       could have made us so vulnerable
   only by patrolling the world

could we have become so hated
       only by fighting so hard
   to preserve the dollar

could we have driven gold
       to ten times its value
   in eleven years

as for those of us
       who are lucky enough
   not to sit hypnotized

our hands on the steering wheel
       which seems to have detached itself
   from the speeding vehicle

it is our job to say
       relax trust
   spend more time with your children

things can only go
       a little better
   if you do not hang on so hard

IV.xiii

O Yava-dvipa
    in the Ramayana
   adorned by seven kingdoms

thronged by gold mines   *Ramayana 4.40.30*
    Iabadiou for Ptolemaeus   'Ιαβαδίου
   an island most fertile

and producing much gold   *Ptolemy 7.2.29*
    O Yeh P'o T'i   耶婆堤
   of the pilgrim Fa Hsien   *Fa Hsien 40; Sarkar 3*

in this country
    heretics and Brahmans flourish   *Beal 168*
   you have believed so often

in adjustment and Nirvana
    the annihilation of the self
   Shiva Sogata rishi   *Sarkar 25*

Shiva and Buddha are one
    in Erlangga's stone inscription
   but different too

Sukarno's Nasakom
    Marxism and God
   blended and blended and blended

to cultivate harmony
    a meeting place
   of all ideologies   *Legge 340-1*

even the PKI   *Indonesian Communist Party*
    looking to warrior heroes
   like Amir Machmud

यवद्वीप

once a PKI cardholder
        now chairman of the DPR   *Parliament*
who arrested Subandrio

the first man I ever met
        at a cocktail party
        to be sentenced to death

(as for calling Amir Machmud
        a CIA agent
        where does it lead?)   *TAPOL 3/86 9*

Yet even Sukarno
        who professed anger
        To hell with your aid

had authorized contracts
        allowing Stanvac and Caltex
        to increase their payments

arranged by a former
        OSS petroleum chief
        and Mobil adviser   *P.D. Scott '75 224*

directly to the accounts
        of Ibnu Sutowo's Permina   *P.D. Scott '85A 254*
        which played a key part

in bankrolling the coup
        according to *Fortune*   *Fortune 7/73 154*
        the army has never forgotten it   *P.D. Scott '75 258*

and which later hired
        the U.S. MILTAG chief
        as Washington lobbyist   *P.D. Scott '85A 255*

and though I used to believe
        Stanvac and Caltex were one
        total programmatic continuity

never the slightest deviation   P.D. Scott '74 98-9
      men from Stanvac and Caltex and Chase
     making OSS contacts

with Ho Chi Minh   P.D. Scott '75 226
      Devadeva Mahadeva   *God of Gods, Great God; Sarkar 35*
     I see now human faces

inwardly consumed
      Texaco the meanest
     and least self-deceiving   *Sampson '76 235-36*

unlike Mobil which
      with only ten percent of Aramco
     consistently wanted more oil   *Sampson '76 204*

hired William Henderson
      old American Friend of Vietnam
     we must be prepared to fight

for Southeast Asia   P.D. Scott '74 127
      and Kenneth Todd Young
     to alert Washington

to Vietnam's *crisis of confidence*   P.D. Scott '74 128
      Schumpeterian gates
     opening to opportunities

of creative destruction
      the writing of Tryksara
     $A + U + M$

on the surface of water   *Sarkar 66*

IV. xiv

He got off the bus and
        strode quickly down the levee
    to an uninhabited area

thirty-five feet below
        called Trinity River bottom
    where he practiced

with his second-hand Mannlicher-Carcano   *McMillan 279*
        wrote Priscilla Johnson
    not bothering to explain

that the man tracing the route
        was not Lee Harvey Oswald
    but a baffled FBI *agent*

almost a year later   *26 WH 61*
        checking out the fourth version
    of Marina's story

as coached by the office-mate
        of Jack Ruby's former attorney
    a senior FBI *informant*

whose meeting with Ruby
        on November 20
    was suppressed by the Warren Commission

and whose partner had been the conduit
        for payoffs from the mob   *P.D. Scott '76 36-37*
    do you understand what I'm saying?

but before I had finished
        the first third of this sentence
    the telephone had been disconnected

no less than four times
        just like six months before
     with the directors of The Fifth Estate

phone call after phone call
        as we hunted in vain
     for the trip words *army intelligence*

Alcohol Tobacco and Firearms Bureau
        or maybe just plain *rifle*
     and the time when Paul's voice

though just ten blocks away
        was like a phone call from Minsk
     I said *give us our sound back please*

and the burst of volume
        sent my ear reeling
     Even the lawyer

for the House Select Committee
        said *I've never heard*
     noises like that on a telephone before

and he never phoned back
        so I can't blame you Gore
     that after the fourth disconnection

I never got the chance
        to proceed with my sentence
     It was Bob Silvers

who explained two days later
        Gore asked me to try from New York
     and the operator said your extension

was not currently in service
        And I can't blame the station
     which stopped phoning for my views

on drugs and the contras
                    after we were cut off
            in the middle of the broadcast

or the bleary-eyed hippie
                    who followed me up Telegraph
            into four or five bookstores

and then back again (until
                    I shook him through a second exit)
            saying over and over

we know who you are
            I work with the FBI
            sooner or later we are going to get you

and I could do nothing about it
            the poor guy
            was so obviously spacy

I can't blame anyone
                    except maybe the advice
            to Odysseus from the blind man

for if a sentence
is left dangling in the mind too long

IV.xv

But when you control
                    most of the world
            you cannot stop

it has been managed before
                    so you are expected
            to manage it again

the cunning plan
        becomes in the streets of Santiago
    a biblical whirlwind

Jakarta is coming
        in *Tribuna* a photograph
    of General Baeza

who led the assault
        on the presidential palace
    when they machine-gunned Allende

holding up in his hand
        the justifying card
    Djakarta se acerca   *Jakarta is approaching*
                                                                      Freed 103-18

mailed to military officers
        to make them believe
    they were scheduled to be liquidated   *P.D. Scott '85A 259*

just as officers in Jakarta
        had been made to believe
    they were scheduled to be liquidated

after the CIA
        in Santiago was instructed
    to *author conclusive evidence*

Allende government
        planned to take country by force
    while the same card

Djakarta se acerca
        had been mailed to leftists
    and published in *El Siglo*

the aim the CIA
        had explained in '61
    was to polarize Laos   *Time 3/17/61*

where Hecksher had been Station Chief
          before presiding in Santiago
     over the so-called *abduction*

of the constitutionalist General Schneider
          and so three years later
     Z

the alleged secret plan
          to murder the chiefs
     of the armed forces

and the formal excuse for the coup   *Freed 117*
          Jakarta Jakarta
     there was no truth wrote David Phillips

to the belief of Mrs. Allende
          whom I know to be a fine person
     that CIA *was behind the coup*   *Phillips 250*

but when we talked
          before the Susskind show
     your right eye twitching

in its efforts to disrupt
          your attempt at a guiltless
     television smile

I could still not bring myself
          to be its accomplice and proclaim
     you murderer liar or even

Chief of WH Division   *Western Hemisphere*
          when CIA *agents*
     in Santiago assisted

in drafting bogus Z-plan
          documents alleging
     that Allende and his supporters

were planning to behead
        Chilean military commanders   *Szulc 724*
    and delle Chiaie's Aginter contacts

appear to have been active   *Laurent 163*
        in the bombings and riots
    of *Patria y Libertad*

supported by Kissinger
        and the 40 Committee   *Dinges 41, 54*
    Djakarta se acerca

before *P y L*
        joined with the military
    in the mop-up brigades

many of whose
        maybe 30,000 victims
    were *tortured to death*

the bodies sometimes
        disfigured beyond recognition   *Amn.Int. 253*
    headless corpses like logs

clogging the Nuble River   *Freed 110*

IV. xvi

For so long
        I have been sitting at my desk
    and I tremble

in front of the terrible blank paper
        the future from which it gathers words
    as the empire

gathers with métèque legions
          around the republic
     to displace its coinage

the earth stirs
          the skies have been opened
          the words must be terrible enough

I have sat on the crag
          above the Rad Lab
     accipiens sonitum

saxi de vertice pastor   *Aen*. 2.307–08
          where it is not hard
     to see the city flattened

after the fires of night
          the only movement
          billowing smoke and dust   *Aen*. 2.609

no people their flesh shall
          consume away
     while they stand upon their feet —   *Zech. 14.12*

this is no more
          than what the record tells us
          Eniwetok the atoll gone

the sky of a thousand suns
          all at once risen   *Bhag. Gita* 11.12
     the fearful mouths

between whose teeth are seen
          the warriors mangled   *Bhag. Gita* 11.17
     writhing without a word

and it is time to go

IV. xvii

And now East Timor
            where in 1977
      the Indonesian minister admits

perhaps 80,000 might have been killed   Chomsky 175
            that is to say one person out of eight
      by his own government's paracommandos

these gentle midnight faces
            the beetles which crowd their eyes
      From 1975 to 1977

the *New York Times* index
            entries for East Timor
      dropped from six columns

to five lines

IV. xviii

And it is easy
            to be introduced
      to Jacques' wife from New York

at Eloise's candlelight
            dinner party and
      say with complete decorum

not like with Gregor *Yes*
            your father was OSS
      Sullivan and Cromwell

and then Standard Oil
            your grandfather
      practiced law with the

son-in-law of J.P. Morgan
            and your cousin here I get
      two completely different

families confused but in vino
            and error I tell truth
      was secretary of the CIA's

Fairfield Foundation
            and his wife's cousin
      Christopher Emmet a descendant

of John Jacob Astor
            and President of the
      American Friends of Vietnam

was the man whose Common Cause
            accepted the tax-deductible   Faenza 297
      donations for the deliverers   P.D. Scott '72 193

of the Marseille waterfront
            into the hands of friendly
      socialists and behind them

the Corsican Guerinis
            already smuggling Saigon opium
      through the Armenians in Beirut

to be sold on Harlem streetcorners
            but why tell you this
      who married a French-Canadian

lawyer from Westmount
            and are serious about the piano
      now it is the new blood

from the Reagan entourage
            who meet with the Aginter
      veterans of the Guatemala bloodbath   Kruger 21

and no one in your
            generation seems to have preserved
        that ancient appetite for power

As long as I haven't
            offended you let
        us step out on the lawn

sloping down to where the
            streetlight in the maples
        at the edge of the water

shines on the long-disused
            lakefront bandstand
        where as a twelve-year-old

I was given popcorn
            to sit still as the
        Voltigeurs de Sherbrooke

went through their precarious
            Saturday-night arousals
        of John Philip Sousa's

martial nostalgia
            What is that whirr
        of low wings in the darkness

of the ornamental pine?
It is the owl

V.i

The village gathers
        for the shadow play
    the Mahabharata or in Kawi

the Barata Yudda
        the Great War
    in which the good Pendawas

return from the forest
        of solitude strong again
    to oust their evil cousins

in a battle so fierce
        the rivers stand still
    the sun pales

and the mountains tremble   *Covarrubias 241*
        just as Oppenheimer
    thought of Vishnu

the sky of a thousand suns   *Bhag. Gita* 11.12
        in the eclipsed shadows
    of Alamogordo

as a man of power
        drawn to the interpolated
    message of Krishna

on the flaming chariot
        standing between the lines
    the eve of the Brahma night   *Bhag. Gita* 8.17

which the *wajang koelit*   *shadow play*
        through centuries of alien
    occupation (the Portuguese

knowing only the word *rapio*)   *May 12*
        makes no mention of
    that the true sage

for whom light is darkness
        will learn from *ahimsa*
    to kill with detachment

to avoid the lawlessness
        leading to corrupted
    family women   *Betai 233-35*

and from this in turn
        to *varnasamkarah*
    intermixture of caste   *Bhag. Gita* 1.40

according to the Gita
        which Gandhi called his *mother*   *Betai i*
    and Dan *Eichman's bible*

(like Joshua's
        Sun stand thou still
    while the Israelis

avenged themselves upon their enemies
        till they were consumed
    that the rest of them

entered fenced cities
        for thus shall the Lord do)   *Joshua 10.12-25*
    first warriors then clowns

the mocking of masters with respect
            the word *act*
        a mountain burning with fire

and the day shone not   *Rev. 8.8,12*
            the forests are dying
        I think of my friend Dan

once first across the paddies
            to hurl his grenade
        into the machine-gun nest

or coming out of the Saigon
            restaurant in black tie
        after leaving Germaine   *'73 Hearings 3886*

saw Michel with a pistol
            reached down and
        scooped sand into his eyes

having already learned
            there were friends for whom he would die
        and no greater glory

vengeance compassion   *Iliad* 24.503; *Aen*. 12.932
            and then detachment
        (detachment not from care

but from the past)
            when he and Allen and the others
        lined up on the railway tracks

at Rocky Flat
            the nuclear warheads plant
        object or subject

you are free to call this
            either witness or theatre
        it was by all means play

and in the final seconds
the train stopped

V. ii

If you bring forth
        what is within you
    it will save you

if you do not bring forth
        what is within you
    it will destroy you   *Gospel of Thomas 45.29-33; Pagels 152*

the papyrus
        removed after two millennia
    from its red jar

and dumped on the straw
        next to the avenger's oven
    by chance not

among those his mother burned
        I read the gnostic
    Gospel of Thomas

and see belatedly
        it was unavoidable
    the saving nausea

the wind-driven angel
        in the all-night tempest
    the blue sea shining

behind the white bones
        of the affable skeleton
    on the painted altarpiece

Morieris et non vives   *You will die and not live*
        in the mountain chapel
    above Lake Como

this smile from my past
        still comes to me
    not those of the scholars

rattling their teacups
        back in the Villa Serbelloni
    alone we go mad

and yet to be human
        is to have this sense
    we are unfit for the crowded maze

and if for a moment
        I am too calm
    at the napalm which descends

on yet another nation
        Steve Carr dead in Van Nuys   *McMichael 7*
    the message for Jack Terrell

you'll be shot
        if you step off that plane
    not my own

inconsiderable death threats
        but that clean morning in Palo Alto
    the former Green Beret

who just the night before
        had said he would talk to us
    about opium in Laos

showing us the sharp black hole
        in his M.G.'s red steel door
    the floorboards hardly scorched

and saying *that hot*
        an imploded thermal charge
      must have come from my old unit

and if from such terror
        we each acknowledge
     we are not normal

in this world where
        we live by forgetting
     as the storm lets up

the white snowflakes dance
        around the streetlamp
     and the flared ghost

once *fleet-footed pursuing*   *Iliad 9.505, 512*
        down the black oak
     still our familiar and yet

if you bring forth
what is within you

              V. iii

Where no vision is
        the people die and yet   *Prov. 29.18*
     it is by imagination's failure

that we go on surviving
        reasonable by day
     and then by night

the nightmare
        where Bisson and Chevalier were ousted
     and they multiply bombs

more than 1200
        nuclear explosions
    since the Jornáda del Muerto

and not since the first
        have there been physicists
    who renounced their clearance

shall I say once again
        why there will be more war
    small and great alike

all are given to gain
        prophet and priest practice fraud   *Jer. 6.13*
    and the people love it   *Jer. 5.31*

yet if we return
        to the old ways
    of the ashvattha tree   *Bhag. Gita* 15.1

fallen fruit in the snow
        small ghost fading in the dawn
    it must be to recognize

not to re-enter
        the fierce gates of the past
    for when the blind woman has seen

the terrible beauty
        of energy come forth
    to destroy the worlds   *Bhag. Gita* 11.32

O Apollo lord of
        the light you blind me   *Agamemnon* 1227
    we cannot like children

go back to duty and *svadharma*   *special or caste duty*
        let there be the courage
    not just to have seen

but to ease into the world
the unreal
breathing within us

SOURCES

Adler, Renata. "Searching for the Real Nixon Scandal." *Atlantic Monthly,* December 1976.

Amnesty International. *Report on Torture.* New York: Farrar, Strauss & Giroux, 1975.

AR: U.S. Congress. House. Select Committee on Assassinations. *Final Report.* Washington, D.C.: GPO, 1979.

Auerbach, Erich. *Literary Language and Its Public.* New York: Pantheon Books, 1965.

Baker, Ray Stannard. *American Chronicle.* New York: Scribner, 1945.

Bateson, Gregory, and Margaret Mead. *Balinese Character.* New York: New York Academy of Sciences, 1942.

Beal, Samuel. *Travels of Fah-Hsian and Sung-Kun, Buddhist Pilgrims, from China to India (400 A.D. and 518 A.D.).* London: Susil Gupta, 1934.

Becker, Elizabeth. *When the War Was Over.* New York: Simon and Schuster, 1986.

Belo, Jane. *Bali: Rangda and Barong.* New York: J. J. Augustin, 1949.

———. *Trance in Bali.* New York: Columbia University Press, 1960.

Berle, Adolf. *Navigating the Rapids.* New York: Harcourt Brace Jovanovich, 1973.

Berlin, Isaiah. *Personal Impressions.* Harmondsworth, Middlesex: Penguin, 1982.

Betai, Ramesh S. *Gita and Gandiji.* Ahmedabad: Gujarat Vidyapith, 1970.

Blum, John Morton. *From the Morgenthau Diaries: Years of Urgency 1938–1941.* Boston: Houghton Mifflin Co., 1965. Revised and condensed in *Roosevelt and Morgenthau.* Boston: Houghton Mifflin Co., 1970.

Brown, Anthony Cave. *The Last Hero: Wild Bill Donovan.* New York: Vintage Books, 1984.

Bulletin of Concerned Asian Scholars. Summer–Fall 1971.

Bullitt, Orville H., ed. *For the President: Personal and Secret.* Boston: Houghton Mifflin Co., 1972.

Chomsky, Noam, and Edward S. Herman. *The Washington Connection and Third World Fascism.* Boston: South End Press, 1979.

Church: See U.S. Congress. Senate. Select Committee to Study Governmental Operations with Respect to Intelligence Activities.

Council on Foreign Relations. *The War and Peace Studies of the Council on Foreign Relations, 1939–1945.* New York, 1946.

Covarrubias, Miguel. *Island of Bali.* New York: Alfred A. Knopf, 1942.

Crouch, Harold. *The Army and Politics in Indonesia.* Ithaca: Cornell University Press, 1978.

Curtius, Ernst Robert. *European Literature and the Latin Middle Ages.* New York: Harper, 1963.

Davies, W.H. *Autobiography of a Supertramp.* New York: Alfred A. Knopf, 1917.

DD: *Declassified Documents.* Carrollton Press.

Dinges, John, and Sol Landau. *Assassination on Embassy Row.* New York: Pantheon Books, 1980.

Djwa, Sandra. *The Politics of the Imagination: A Life of F.R. Scott.* Toronto: McClelland and Stewart, 1987.

Doyle, Kevin. "Prince Who Fell from Grace." *Atlas,* December 1976.

Dulles, John Foster. *War, Peace and Change.* New York: Harper and Brothers, 1939.

Duroselle, Jean-Baptiste. *From Wilson to Roosevelt.* New York: Harper and Row, 1968.

Erikson, Erik H. *Gandhi's Truth: On the Origins of Militant Nonviolence.* New York: W.W. Norton, 1969.

Faenza, Roberto, and Marco Fini. *Gli Americani in Italia.* Milan: Feltrinelli, 1976.

Fairbank, John. "Comment." *Bulletin of Concerned Asian Scholars.* Summer–Fall 1971.

Fifield, Russell H. *Southeast Asia in United States Policy.* New York: Frederick A. Praeger, for the Council on Foreign Relations, 1963.

Freed, Donald, with Fred Landis. *Death in Washington.* Westport, Conn.: Lawrence Hill, 1980.

Geertz, Clifford. *Peddlers and Princes.* Chicago: University of Chicago Press, 1963.

———. *The Interpretation of Cultures.* New York: Basic Books, 1973.

———. *Negara.* Princeton: Princeton University Press, 1980.

Girard, Rene. Translated by Patrick Gregory. *Violence and the Sacred.* Baltimore: Johns Hopkins Press, 1977.

Hamburger, Michael, and Christopher Middleton. *Modern German Poetry 1910–1960.* New York: Grove Press, 1960.

Hearings: See U.S. Congress.

Homans, George C. "Commentary on Schlesinger." *American Sociological Review*, February 1963. In *The Structure of Evil* by Ernest Becker. New York: The Free Press, 1968.

———. *The Human Group*. New York: Harcourt, Brace and World, 1950.

Hoopes, Townsend. *The Devil and John Foster Dulles*. Boston: Little, Brown, 1973.

Hougan, Jim. *Spooks*. New York: William Morrow, 1978.

Hudson, Michael. *Super Imperialism*. New York: Holt, Rinehart & Winston, 1972.

Ignatieff, George. *The Memoirs of George Ignatieff: The Making of a Peacemonger*. Toronto: University of Toronto Press, 1985.

Kaplan, Justin. *Lincoln Steffens: a Biography*. New York: Simon and Schuster, 1974.

Kartawidjaja [Pipit Rochijat]. Translated by Ben Anderson. "Am I PKI or Non-PKI?" *Indonesia*, October 1985.

Kolko, Gabriel. *The Politics of War: The World and United States Foreign Policy, 1943–1945*. New York: Random House, 1968.

Krause, Gregor. *Bali*. Munich: Georg Muller, 1926.

Kruger, Henrik. *The Great Heroin Coup*. Boston: South End Press, 1980.

Kwitny, Jonathan. *The Crimes of Patriots*. New York: W.W. Norton, 1987.

Kytle, Calvin. *Gandhi, Soldier of Nonviolence*. New York: Grosset and Dunlap, 1969.

Laurent, Frédéric. *L'Orchestre noir*. Paris: Stock, 1978.

Lee, Martin, and Bruce Shlain. *Acid Dreams: The CIA, LSD and the Sixties Rebellion*. New York: Grove Press, 1985.

Legge, J. D. *Sukarno: A Political Biography*. London: Allen Lane: The Penguin Press, 1972.

Lernoux, Penny. *In Banks We Trust*. Garden City, N.Y.: Anchor Press/Doubleday, 1984.

Lippmann, Walter. *The Phantom Public*. New York: Macmillan, 1930.

Mailer, Norman. *The Armies of the Night*. New York: New American Library, 1968.

Mandelstam, Nadezhda. *Hope Against Hope: A Memoir*. New York: Atheneum, 1979.

Marshall, Jonathan V. "Bankers and the Search for a Separate Peace During World War II." Master's thesis, Cornell University, 1981.

————, Peter Dale Scott, and Jane Hunter. *The Iran-Contra Connection.* Boston, South End Press, 1987.

May, Brian. *The Indonesian Tragedy.* London: Routledge and Kegan Paul, 1978.

[McMichael, David.] *Crime and the Contras—A Summary Report.* Washington: International Center for Development Policy, [1986].

McMillan, Priscilla Johnson. *Marina and Lee.* New York: Harper and Row, 1978.

Morton, Frederic. *The Rothschilds.* New York: Fawcett, n.d.

Mosley, Leonard. *Dulles.* New York: The Dial Press/James Wade, 1978.

Mrázek, Rudolf. *The United States and the Indonesian Military 1945–1965: A Study of an Intervention.* 2nd vol. Prague: Academia, 1978.

Naylor, R.T. *Hot Money and the Politics of Debt.* New York: Linden Press/Simon and Schuster, 1987.

Pagels, Elaine. *The Gnostic Gospels.* New York: Random House, 1979.

Pauker, Guy J. *Communist Prospects in Indonesia.* Santa Monica: RAND Corporation, RM-5753-PR, November 1964.

————. "The Role of the Military in Indonesia." In *The Role of the Military in Underdeveloped Countries,* edited by John J. Johnson. Princeton: Princeton University Press, 1962.

Payne, Robert. *The Life and Death of Mahatma Gandhi.* London: Bodley Head, 1969.

PP: *The Pentagon Papers: The Defense Department History of United States Decisionmaking on Vietnam.* Boston: Beacon Press, 1971.

Phillips, David Atlee. *The Night Watch.* New York: Atheneum, 1977.

Powers, Thomas. *The War at Home.* New York: Grossman, 1973.

Ransom, David. "Ford Country." In *The Trojan Horse,* edited by Steve Weissman. San Francisco: Ramparts Press, 1974.

Reid, Ed, and Ovid Demaris. *The Green Felt Jungle.* New York: Pocket Books, 1964.

Sampson, Anthony. *The Arms Bazaar.* New York: Viking, 1977.

————. *The Seven Sisters.* New York: Viking, 1975.

Sarkar, Himansu Bhusan. *Indian Influences on the Literature of Java and Bali.* Calcutta: Greater India Society, 1934.

Schurmann, Franz. *The Logic of World Power.* New York: Pantheon Books, 1974.

————, Peter Dale Scott, and Reginald Zelnik. *The Politics of Escalation in Vietnam.* New York: Fawcett, 1966.

Scott, F. R. *Collected Poems.* Toronto: McClelland and Stewart, 1981.

Scott, Frank R. *A New Endeavour: Selected Political Essays, Letters, and Addresses.* Edited by Michiel Horn. Toronto: University of Toronto Press, 1986.

Scott, Frederick George. *The Great War as I Saw It.* Vancouver: Clarke and Stuart, 1934.

Scott, Peter Dale. *Crime and Cover-Up: the CIA, the Mafia, and the Dallas-Watergate Connection.* Berkeley: Westworks, 1976.

————. "Exporting Military-Economic Development." In *Ten Years' Military Terror in Indonesia,* edited by Malcolm Caldwell. Nottingham: Spokesman Books, 1975.

————. "The United States and the Overthrow of Sukarno." *Pacific Affairs,* Summer 1985.

————. "De Verenigde Staten & Indonesie 1965." In *Indonesie: De Waarheid Omtrent 1965.* Amsterdam: Indonesia Media, 1985.

————. "The Vietnam War and the CIA-Financial Establishment." In *Remaking Asia: Essays on the American Uses of Power,* edited by Mark Seldon. New York: Pantheon Books, 1974.

————. *The War Conspiracy.* Indianapolis and New York: Bobbs Merrill, 1972.

Shaplen, Robert. *Time Out of Hand.* New York: Harper and Row, 1969.

Shoup, Lawrence H., and William Minter. *Imperial Brain Trust.* New York: Monthly Review Press, 1977.

Smith, R. Harris. *OSS.* Berkeley: University of California Press, 1972.

Smith, Walter Buckingham. *Economic Aspects of the Second Bank of the United States.* Cambridge: Harvard University Press, 1953.

Stock, Noel. *The Life of Ezra Pound.* San Francisco: North Point Press, 1982.

Szulc, Tad. *The Illusion of Peace.* New York: Viking, 1978.

U.S. Congress. House. Committee on Government Operations. *Oversight Hearings into the Operations of the IRS (Operation Tradewinds, Project Haven, and Narcotics Traffickers Tax Program), Hearings.* Washington, D.C.: GPO, 1975.

————. Senate. Committee on Foreign Relations. *Multinational Corporations and United States Foreign Policy, Hearings,* Part XII. Washington, D.C.: GPO, 1976.

————. Senate. Committee on the Judiciary. *Institute of Pacific Relations, Hearings*. Washington, D.C.: GPO, 1952.

————. Senate. Select Committee to Study Governmental Operations with Respect to Intelligence Activities. *Foreign and Military Intelligence*, Report No. 94-755, Book I. Washington, D.C.: GPO, 1976.

————. Senate. Select Committee on Presidential Campaign Activities. *Presidential Campaign Activities of 1972: Senate Resolution 60, Hearings*. Washington, D.C.: GPO, 1973.

Van Dusen, Henry P. *The Spiritual Legacy of John Foster Dulles*. Philadelphia: Westminster Press, 1960.

WH: U.S., Warren Commission. *Hearings*. Washington, D.C.: GPO, 1964.

Wisely, William. *A Tool of Power: The Political History of Money*. New York: John Wiley and Sons, 1977.

de Zoete, Beryl and Walter Spies. *Dance and Drama in Bali*. Kuala Lumpur and London: Oxford University Press, 1973.

AUTHOR'S NOTE

In the nine years since I first wrote this poem in October 1980, many more people have helped than I can name here, above all my colleagues, students, and other friends at Berkeley. I must mention especially Janine Canan and the group of poets who used to meet with the late Josephine Miles; thanks also to Robert Pinsky, Robert Hass, and Frank Bidart who helped the poem towards its eventual publication, as did Ron Graham and Michael Ondaatje in Canada. For editorial and other assistance in the poem's final stages I must thank Laura Morland, Ellen Seligman, Russell Brown, James Schamus, Nancy Kricorian, and Vic Marks of the Typeworks.

In 1983 I read much of the poem to Robert Hass's poetry workshop in Berkeley. A week later I received in the mail an extensive, anonymous critique of the poem, offering line-by-line appreciations and emendations. For six months I knew only that there existed someone who had puzzled out some of the poem's mechanics, better at times than I had myself.

Then by good fortune I encountered at a reception this unknown editor, Kim Maltman, and his close friend Roo Borson. The two, well-known Canadian poets, have continued over the years to sharpen my awareness of what this poem is up to, and even on occasion to present themselves as my Muse's attorneys. I have accepted enough of their many suggestions to make *Coming to Jakarta*, in a strangely rewarding way, no longer wholly my own.

(Because Kim is also a particle physicist, the poem, which ends with evocations of Oppenheimer's Hindu apocalypse, ironically received its final editing sessions amid minatory thunder and hailstorms in Los Alamos, the University of California weapons facility in New Mexico.)

I hope soon to finish revising this poem's sequel, *Listening to the Candle: A Poem on Impulse*, dedicated to my mother, Marian Dale Scott.

Coming to Jakarta was originally published in Canada in 1988 by McClelland and Stewart of Toronto. Four sections were included in Number 11 of the Reed Foundation Poetry Chapbook Series, published by the Dia Art Foundation of New York, in connection with a reading there in January 1989. Portions have also appeared in *The Berkeley Graduate*, the *Berkeley Poetry Review*, *Berkeley U.S.A.* by Anne Moose, *Epoch, Ironwood, Witness*, and the anthology *'What Thou Lovest Well Remains': 100 Years of Ezra Pound*, ed. Richard Ardinger.

A PARTIAL CHRONOLOGY

1957   CIA approves direct aid to rebel Indonesian army colonels.

3/14/57   Partly in response to U.S.-subsidized regional dissension, Indonesian President Sukarno declares martial law.

5/18/58   CIA pilot shot down and captured in Sumatra.

8/1/58   U.S. begins upgraded program of military assistance to Indonesian Army as "encouragement" to carry out plan "for the control of Communism."

8/59   RAND Conference on "The Role of the Military in Underdeveloped Countries." Guy Pauker urges Indonesian Army to carry out "a control function."

1959–60   Council on Foreign Relations Study Group on Southeast Asia, followed in 1963 by Prof. Fifield's book.

3/22/61   CIA memo expresses frustration with pro-Sukarno record of Indonesian Army General Nasution.

12/18/63   Incoming President Johnson withholds economic aid to Indonesia.

1962–65   U.S. cuts back on military aid to Indonesia, except to selected anti-Sukarno elements of Army.

1965   1958 CIA rebel contact visits Washington, recommends Suharto as new leader for Indonesia.

5/65   Intelligence-controlled Lockheed payoffs to Indonesian influence-men redirected to Suharto's financial backer, General Alamsjah.

7/65   Secret contract to deliver U.S. planes for "civic action" to Indonesian Army.

9/65   Indonesian generals warned of impending assassination plots. Planted stories abroad speak of arms-smuggling to Java from mainland China.

9/30/65	Jani and his pro-Sukarno supporters on Army General Staff are rounded up and murdered. Nasution escapes.
10/1/65	Massacre of Communists and ethnic Chinese begins. Suharto takes over, closes all papers except Communist and one other on left.
10/2/65	Questioned issue of Communist paper supports alleged coup attempt of September 30; becomes pretext to continue massacre.
10–12/65	RPKAD Commandos of Col. Sarwo Edhie spread massacre to other parts of Indonesia. More than 500,000 killed.
3/11/66	Suharto arrests pro-Sukarno ministers in partial coup.
6/19/66	James Reston in *New York Times* describes "Indonesian massacre" as "A Gleam of Light in Asia."
3/13/67	Suharto announces that Sukarno is no longer President.
1967	Richard Nixon reportedly tells U.S. Ambassador to Indonesia that "Indonesian experience" shows how "we should handle our relationships on a wider basis . . . in the world."
1973	CIA agents in Chile help draft bogus documents alleging that Allende plans to behead military commanders. Small cards distributed with words *Djakarta se acerca* ("Jakarta is approaching").
1981	Former CIA agent Ralph McGehee reveals CIA deception operation for Indonesia in 1965, designed to set the stage for a massacre.

ABOUT THE AUTHOR

Peter Dale Scott was born in 1929 in Montreal, Canada. He studied at McGill University (B.A., 1949), the Institut D'Etudes Politiques, Paris (1950), and University College, Oxford (1950–52), before receiving his Ph.D. in Political Science from McGill in 1955. In 1953 he taught at Sedbergh School, Montebello, Quebec. In 1956 he married Maylie Marshall; they have three children. From 1957 to 1961 he was a Canadian diplomat, serving at the United Nations General Assembly, and for two years in Warsaw, Poland. Since 1961 he has taught at the University of California, Berkeley, where he is now a Professor of English. While at Berkeley he became involved in the anti-Vietnam War movement, as a result of which he has published books dealing with the Vietnam War and the assassination of John F. Kennedy: *The Politics of Escalation in Vietnam* (in collaboration); *The War Conspiracy; The Assassinations: Dallas and Beyond* (in collaboration); and *Crime and Cover-Up*. His most recent prose book is *The Iran-Contra Connection,* co-authored with Jonathan Marshall and Jane Hunter (Boston: South End Press, 1987 and Montreal: Black Rose Books, 1987). In the realm of poetry, he has published *Poems* (Oxford: Fantasy Press, 1952); *Rumors of No Law* (Austin, Tex.: Thorp Springs Press, 1980); *Prepositions of Jet Travel* (Berkeley: Berkeley Poetry Review, 1981); and *Heart's Field* (Berkeley: Aroca Press, 1986). His translations (with Czeslaw Milosz) of the Polish poet Zbigniew Herbert were first published in 1968 and recently reissued. *Coming to Jakarta* was completed while he was a visiting Senior Fellow at the International Center for Development Policy, Washington, D.C.